the WELL-TEMPERED *life*

the WELL-TEMPERED life

Coach Yourself to Wellness

Walking The Tightrope: A Personal Balancing Act

R. Danielle Gault

NEW YORK

the WELL-TEMPERED *life*
Coach Yourself to Wellness
© 2012 R. Danielle Gault. All rights reserved.

ISBN 978-1-61448-182-9 Paperback
ISBN 978-1-61448-183-6 eBook
Library of Congress Control Number: 2012932321

Morgan James Publishing
The Entrepreneurial Publisher
5 Penn Plaza, 23rd Floor,
New York City, New York 10001
(212) 655-5470 office • (516) 908-4496 fax
www.MorganJamesPublishing.com

For information, please contact:
Wellness Training Services
www.corporate-training-services.com

Editorial Support by
Brian Parsons
Swift Solutions
Technical Support by
Bill Gault
Cover Design by:
Rachel Lopez
www.r2cdesign.com
Interior Design by:
Bonnie Bushman
bonnie@caboodlegraphics.com

Photo Credits: 29, upper middle dbartone/istockphoto.com • 29, lower middle Dzmitry Stankevich/bigstockphoto.com • 29, bottom Morgan James • 35, left Dmitrijs Gerciks/bigstockphoto.com • 35, right Dmitrijs Gerciks/bigstockphoto.com • 36, left Lev Dolgachov/bigstockphoto.com • 36, right Leah-Anne Thompson/bigstockphoto.com • 53 Antonina Tsyganko/bigstockphoto.com • 109, top Dmitrijs Gerciks/bigstockphoto.com • 109, bottom Robert Lerich/bigstockphoto.com • 110 Lev Olkha/bigstockphoto.com

In an effort to support local communities, raise awareness and funds, Morgan James Publishing donates a percentage of all book sales for the life of each book to Habitat for Humanity Peninsula and Greater Williamsburg.

Habitat
for Humanity®
Peninsula and
Greater Williamsburg
Building Partner

Get involved today, visit
www.MorganJamesBuilds.com.

Table of Contents

Preface

I remember the awe and mystery of the natural healing arts when I first started to explore them. There seemed to be so much information that I was often overwhelmed and confused. Sometimes skepticism accompanied the thrill I felt as I acquired this new knowledge. I took in information, learned how to work with it, and tried for a while to apply it; only once I experienced results did I believe in it.

Personality theory, coaching techniques, yoga, and reflexology— healing modalities for mind, body, and health—are tools and teachings I valued the most and have continued to work with for more than three decades. Using these tools and teachings, I have witnessed amazing results. I have seen people experience improved health, reduced pain, increased well-being, and renewed empowerment.

This self-help book relates coaching techniques, yoga, and reflexology to the personality elements of AIR, FIRE, WATER, and EARTH, providing ways to use self-knowledge and healing methods to bring balance to your life. These tools and techniques can help your mind, body, and soul to navigate your journey toward a well-tempered life—a life that is shaped, refined, and honed to express its highest purpose.

Disclaimer: *This book suggests strategies to reduce stress and increase relaxation. Always consult your health-care professional before undertaking any self-help suggestions. Always work within your own personal comfort level.*

Acknowledgments

My heartfelt thanks to my husband for his continuous love, patience, and support; to the many teachers who are brave enough to share their knowledge and wisdom with others; and especially to Dr. Mishra for his teachings on how to learn from and enjoy the drama and game of life.

PART I

TOOLS FOR A
WELL-TEMPERED LIFE

This section introduces elemental personality theory, yoga, and reflexology. These are coaching tools that can help your mind, body, and soul to navigate your journey to a well-tempered life—a life that is shaped, refined, and honed to express its highest purpose.

*Tempered: possessing both the hardiness
and the flexibility needed to be resilient*

CHAPTER 1

ELEMENTAL PERSONALITY THEORY

R ecently I was interviewed about coaching on a radio show:

HOST: *Danielle, let's assume that life on planet Earth is a game. If this is so, there must be some rules and tools. What are the rules and tools that you would use for this game?*

ME: *The first rule is the requirement for us to be self-aware. Then tools for gaining insights and developing strategies can be applied to help us to stay both hardy and flexible when dealing with the events in life so that we are always resilient.*

Without self-awareness, without a conscious approach to life, it is like driving through a city using the wrong map. If you apply the wrong map, no matter how good you are at reading it or how skilled you are at driving, you will not get to where you want to go. To coach yourself to wellness and to maintain balance in your life, you must have self-awareness and be able to answer the questions: "Who am I?" and "Where do I want to go?"

You have to understand yourself, your strengths and your weaknesses, in order to master the game of life and to create the best outcome in any given situation or context.

This book is designed to assist you in understanding and interpreting your world. You will learn guidelines and a set of tools to enhance your insights, skills, and techniques as you navigate your journey in life and strive to coach yourself always toward balance—no matter what your age, stage, or situation. We are all navigating, negotiating, and striving to stay healthy, well, and balanced; having a few guidelines and tools at our fingertips can assist us. Throughout the book I will link the personality elements to coaching tips and the healing techniques of yoga and reflexology.

My recommendation is to use the ideas, techniques, and tools as you see fit, but do keep in mind that life is dynamic and not meant to be easy: We are all striving to satisfy our human needs as we bump up against others who are also playing the same game, striving to satisfy theirs.

Identifying and working with your personality preference can aid you in maximizing your strengths and avoiding your pitfalls. Elemental personality theory works with four types of awareness. These awarenesses could be called the *mental* awareness, the *social-mental* awareness, the *social-physical* awareness, and the *physical* awareness. Each of these awarenesses helps to guide us through life by taking on a specific responsibility.

PERSONALITY PREFERENCES

The mental awareness deals with thoughts and ideas. The social-mental awareness deals with connections to the ideas. The social-physical awareness deals with a broader range of connections to people, things, and feelings than the social-mental. The physical awareness deals with doing and manifesting results. Although we all use all of the awarenesses, we each generally prefer to use one awareness over the others. We tend to want to stay in our preferred choice and use it more often, thereby developing and making it easily accessible to us. And because of this, we tend to take it for granted, even discounting its value in our life: It is easy for us to use as along the way we have made distinctions on how to apply it and when to apply it through many trials and errors.

The work of Dr. Carl Gustav Jung has been influential in the development of personality theory. In *Psychological Types*,[1] he said that what appears to be random behavior in people is really consistent behavior over time. He also stated that our preference for how we take in and relate to information is inherent in us. Inherent tendencies can be illustrated through our preference for using the left or right hand when writing. We prefer one hand to the other, so it is used more often and our handwriting becomes well developed, flows easily and appears mature.

When asked to use the opposite hand to write our signature, we find that we need more concentration, it takes more effort and energy and often the results appear immature and messy.

Experience what I mean in the following exercise.

_____

Write your signature as you usually do.

_____

Now, write your signature using your other hand.

---

1   Jung, C.G. *Psychological Types*. Bollingen Series XX, Volume 6. Princeton University Press. 1976.

Of course you can write with your opposite hand, but it probably felt awkward and took more concentration, and the result may not even be legible.

Our use of awarenesses, like handwriting, is similar in that it is an inherent preference, and once developed, shows up as our dominant expression when living and working in our world with and through others. On teams, we will want to focus more on one awareness over the others. We think that our preference is the most important point of any team project or assignment. In families, we think we have the answers for our children or mates because we are so used to seeing the world through our own lens. What we need to do is expand our lens so that we can see the world from a broader perspective and have more options. This is a main emphasis of this book: to provide you with more options when striving to maintain balance in your life.

MORE ABOUT OUR AWARENESSES

MENTAL AWARENESS. The mind, as the objective part of ourselves, receives intuitive information and then analytically and logically attempts to organize our experiences. The mental awareness gathers an overview, sees the general structures, and assists us in establishing a framework for our values and expectations about our life. We often think of this awareness as the Dreamer, which provides us with our vision. Because the mental awareness does not concern itself with the limitations of the physical awareness or with the feelings and connections of the social awareness, it can float freely upward above the forms and feelings.

Like the element of AIR, it is all seeing and everywhere, yet it is unseen. When ideas come pouring forth, they inspire us, make us excited, and propel us into having further thoughts.

SOCIAL AWARENESS. There are two types and functions for the social awareness. There is the social-mental and the social-physical. Both address the personal parts of our nature and strive to connect ideas to things and people.

The social-mental awareness functions as the Realist and in an outward and upward direction, connecting actions to the ideas of the mental awareness.

The social-physical awareness functions as the Catalyst in us, and in an outward and downward direction connects reactions and feelings to the ideas of the Dreamer and the actions of the Realist to the physical awareness.

In this way, both social awarenesses act in a co-functional manner, and both together become the interface between the ideas of the mental function and the manifestation of the ideas in the physical world.

The social-mental awareness sees the ideas of the Dreamer and feels the tension to move ideas into actions. This tension creates a motivation for action. When the drive to achieve interacts with the events in its current reality, it confronts and deals with obstacles as if they were annoyances to be eliminated. In striving to connect actions to ideas, the Realist often stirs and unsettles us; we feel alert and attentive.

We think of the social-mental process of connecting ideas to actions as the element of FIRE because the actions heat things up, causing friction within as well as with others as it heightens our focus and illuminates the creative processes for others to consider.

The social-physical awareness connects the ideas of the Dreamer and the actions of the Realist to personal reactions and feelings of doubt and concern. These feelings force the need for clarification and assistance in shaping and reshaping the whole process toward its conclusion or outcome. This function is called the Catalyst because it brings thoughts and feelings to the surface so that they can be dealt with.

We think of the social-physical process of connecting both ideas and actions with people and things as the element of WATER. Ideas and actions now start to take shape as other people and things are drawn into the process.

PHYSICAL AWARENESS. As the practical side of ourselves, the physical gross sense perceptions include hearing, seeing, touching, smelling, and tasting. We use our sensate reality to build, make, and manifest tangible results in the physical world. The physical awareness strives to manifest the ideas, actions, and reactions of the other three awarenesses.

Of all of these awarenesses, the physical awareness has the most concern of all the others on the details, distinctions, and refinements of the end result. As it strives to ensure that ideas are manifested, it looks for what is missing and acts as the Critic. Because it is practical and aware of parameters and limitations, it kicks into action only when all the pieces are clearly in place.

The physical awareness is interested in the end product and the final result, and builds downward, creating solid outcomes. We think of the physical process as the element of EARTH as it concretizes the ideas of the Dreamer with the actions of the Realist and the reactions of the Catalyst to produce the outcome initiated by the mental awareness.

The Dreamer, the Realist, the Catalyst, and the Critic operate as a whole system whereby the social process (social-mental and social-physical) serves as the interface between the mental and physical processes.

In a metaphorical sense, the social-mental awareness uses the process of FIRE to go to where the Dreamer in us resides. In order to get a focus or goal, it taps into our mental awareness of AIR. It then comes down to the social-mental level and translates the goal or focus into immediate action steps.

The social-physical awareness, on the other hand, using the process of WATER, goes down to the physical awareness or EARTH and assists in the assimilation of manifesting the idea.

The elements of FIRE and WATER are the interface between AIR and EARTH. AIR and EARTH, being such different expressions—one intangible and the other tangible—are worlds apart, and without an interface they would lack the ability for integrative growth and development.

AWARENESS	ELEMENT	FUNCTION	DIRECTION
Mental	AIR	Dreamer	Upward
Social-mental	FIRE	Realist	Outward and upward
Social-physical	WATER	Catalyst	Outward and downward
Physical	EARTH	Critic	Downward

THE HUMAN INSTRUMENT

Although all four awarenesses operate within each of us, our preferred and dominant awareness filters how we begin to process information. For example, the AIR element sees new ideas first, the FIRE element longs for actions first, the WATER element feels reactions first, and the

EARTH element initially sees all the problems inherent in building a project or completing a goal.

DOMINANT ELEMENTS IN ACTION

Here are some examples of element combinations:

- If the dominant AIR element has as its secondary process EARTH, the focus will be on theory first and the practical side of the theory second. If EARTH is first and AIR is second, the reverse would be true. Consideration for FIRE and WATER elements are often forgotten or minimized and little thought is given to the impact of decisions on others.

- When the FIRE element is first and the AIR element is second, an idea is run with and put into action—and nothing had better get in the way or "rain on the parade." Things get done quickly, although not always effectively since the responses are only to current data without the considerations of past experience and more detailed information. If AIR is first and FIRE is second, the focus is on theory with strong reactions to criticism or obstacles to expressing the theory. Moving quickly from one project or activity to another, there is little tolerance of WATER and EARTH expressions— and taking care of the physical body may be neglected or forgotten.

- When the FIRE element has EARTH as its second element, there will be a striving to be in perpetual action. While focusing on controlling sensate and practical outcomes, there will be a tendency to bulldoze others in getting things done. When EARTH is first and FIRE is second, there will be a tendency to over-control events and over-parent people. Lack of tolerance for AIR and WATER can often alienate others, causing a team or family to break down.

- When the WATER element is first and AIR is second, there is the tendency to be the philosopher who continuously seeks personal meaning to life. When AIR is first and WATER is second, the philosopher strives to right the wrongs of the world through an intellectual abstract process. Failing to deal with the realities of life, there can be a lack of understanding of the practical results-driven qualities of FIRE and EARTH and often an inability to build appropriate boundaries and deal adequately with issues.

PATHWAY TO INCREASED SELF-AWARENESS

Our least preferred awarenesses, and therefore our least developed element, provides our pathway to increased self-awareness. This is because this element lies below the surface of our attention and creates a slight tension in us as it attempts to be felt and surfaced. This inner tension aids us in "staying awake" for developing ourselves more fully. When we do not respond to this tension, we become arrested in our personal development. Others often experience us as boring and stagnant.

Some people try to shortcut their personal development by attaching themselves to others who hold the qualities of the element that they lack. Often this happens in marriages. However, as the union continues, the qualities that were once seen as appealing become irritating. There is no shortcut to personal development. To be fully developed, we require the ability to draw on all our awarenesses and use all our elements. Following is an example of the need for continual development:

When a father prefers the mental awareness and the use of the AIR element, he tends to look at systems and take an overview. If he combines

AIR with a secondary preference for the physical awareness of EARTH, he will have a strong need to see and control work-related and family-related activities of others. He may act like a military general in running his household. Because he lacks a well-developed social awareness, he is not interested in social connections and the feelings of others. His family members tend to move away from him as they grow older and are removed from his control. Once the father/general no longer has a "camp," he looks around and finds that no one wants to be there for him when he starts to develop emotional needs later in life. Then, when he attempts to make connections that would help him in developing his social awareness, he often finds that he has alienated his family and feels abandoned.

When we look at personality preferences, it pays to remember that we are only discussing preferences. We are not trying to typecast people, but rather to understand their needs. These preferences, like any subjective analysis, are designed to give us insight. They are not meant to box us into a set category. Using a model of understanding, the human instrument can provide us with an objective analysis using the idea of AIR, FIRE, WATER, and EARTH to help us focus on our natural strengths and gifts as well as become more aware of our pitfalls or blind spots.

PITFALLS OF IMMATURELY EXPRESSED PREFERENCES

Each element has gifts that it strives to share with the world. Without developing a full understanding of ourselves, these gifts can be expressed immaturely and become personal liabilities, pitfalls, or blind spots. If we fail to address and learn from the painful struggles that these underdeveloped processes can create, then we arrest our own personal growth.

- When people are too much AIR, we experience them as having unrealistic expectations. Always living within an overview and without a realistic sense of the detailed physical world, AIR-preferred people are forever escalating their standards for achieving results. They seem to be never satisfied. We grow tired of these people and move away from them. Because we can never meet their demands, our own self-esteem can suffer.

To stand up to these people, we need to have a clear understanding of how their behavior affects us and be able to articulate problems in a way that is respectful of their needs, the outcome, and ourselves. If these people are unwilling to work with us on the resolution of this problem, then we best pull away.

For example, to let them know how they are affecting us, we could say:

"When there is no end in sight, I feel that we are never going to accomplish anything solid, and that I am never good enough at what I'm doing. Can we discuss milestones and a way to recognize our accomplishments so I can feel satisfied with the work I'm doing?"

- When people are too much FIRE, we experience them as intense and dominating. They can cause too much friction and discomfort. When we are around people who are moving too fast, we feel forced to speed up our own processes and we can become exhausted or burned out. We tend to move away from immature FIRE people because we feel that our needs will not be honored. We should strive to inform these people of the impact their behavior has on us.

For example, if they tend to speak fast and loudly, we could say:

"When you speak fast and loudly, it triggers a feeling in me of being wrong, and then I find it difficult to speak up for myself. Can we work out a method of communicating without raising our voices so that I can stay engaged with you?"

- When people are too much WATER, we experience them as being overly sensitive, taking everything too personally, and bogging us down with all their processing of feelings. We soon grow tired of feeling as if we have to walk around on eggshells. We tend to want to avoid these people and look for more stimulating and productive interactions with others.

For example, when they take us off track, we could say:

"Spending so much time on our feelings is causing me to lose my focus on the job and getting the results we are after. Can we get back on track and place our attention on what we are here to do?"

- When people are too much EARTH, we experience them as holding us back because they are stuck in old systems that have outlived their purpose. Tired of beating our heads against a brick wall, we move on and eventually leave them behind, mocking them for their stick-in-the-mud approach to life. We should inform them that sometimes change is good for a project and has to be considered.

For example, when it is difficult to turn around their position, we could say:

"Would you be willing to consider talking about a somewhat different approach? We have some ideas we would like to pass by you and we would like to get your opinion. What do you think?"

The following chart summarizes key items of elements and awarenesses.

DREAMER / REALIST / CATALYST / CRITIC	
DREAMER – AIR **MENTAL** Connects ideas to imagination and possibilities. Sees overview. Creativity-driven; finds new viewpoints. **SEEKS:** Knowledge **NEEDS:** Respect for competencies honed	**REALIST – FIRE** **SOCIAL-MENTAL** Connects facts to experience and to immediate practical actions. Solutions-driven; finds answers to problems. **SEEKS:** Freedom and action **NEEDS:** Respect for solutions achieved
CATALYST – WATER **SOCIAL-PHYSICAL** Connects emotions to experience; is subjective and idealistic. Subjective-driven; sees and wants to develop potential in others. **SEEKS:** Meaningful life **NEEDS:** Respect for human expression	**CRITIC – EARTH** **PHYSICAL** Connects details to experience and to cause and effect. Analytical-driven; sees problems and what is missing. **SEEKS:** Perfect results **NEEDS:** Respect for practical applications

As we journey through life, it is important that we develop the qualities of all the elements while at the same time we recognize and honor our most preferred. Jung said that our dominant preference is like the captain of our ship. However, we need to use the other crewmembers when they are required, so we do need to develop them. In developing them, Jung says that we then engage in a process he called "individuation," which means that we become more integrated, whole, fully developed, and mature expressions of ourselves.

WHICH AWARENESS IS MOST LIKE YOU?

Here is a short quiz to help you to find out about yourself and your primary awareness. For each of the nine statements, distribute ten points among the four options given according to your degree of preference.

1. When I start a project, I focus first on:
    a. the overview, considering the systems involved in order to get a sense of where I am going.
    b. the compelling need to take the project and run with it in order to get things moving quickly.
    c. who else can be included in the project as well as where to reach out and pull in useful resources.
    d. finding a part of the project that I can work on.
2. When I work with others, it is important for me to know:
    a. how knowledgeable and competent others are.
    b. how quickly others can get on with their tasks and leave me to act on my own senses.
    c. how comfortable others are in sharing their feelings while engaging with me to get the job done.
    d. how timely and consistent others are in following the rules and completing their tasks.
3. When considering ideas, I tend to:
    a. need to understand the underlying principles.

b. like to do what feels most interesting and exciting.

c. take on the ideas and concerns of others.

d. look for what is practical.

4. When working with others, I often:

a. engage in a self-critical process as if what I am doing could always be better.

b. think that the actions I am taking are what is needed at the moment.

c. think that positive, constructive feedback is critical to the group dynamics.

d. have a need for service to the whole group.

5. When in discussions with others, I prefer to:

a. engage in logical reasoning.

b. debate ideas in a passionate manner.

c. ensure that everyone is involved.

d. engage deeply in things that I know a great deal about or otherwise I tend to be reticent.

6. In general, I would prefer to focus mostly on:

a. the future and what is possible.

b. the present and what is immediately needed.

c. the processes rather than on time in general.

d. the past and what it can teach about today.

7. The most important thing to me would be that I am recognized for:

a. my knowledge and competencies.

b. my immediate solutions and quick problem-solving processes.

c. my abilities to tap into and develop the strengths of others.

d. my detailed solutions and thorough problem-solving processes.

8. If I could find the ideal occupation it would it be:

   a. on the senior management team of a leading-edge organization.

   b. in the communications and/or marketing division of an organization.

   c. in the human resources and/or employee relations division of an organization.

   d. in the information technology, design, accounting, or production divisions of an organization.

9. If I had to choose the most important motivator that helps me to navigate my life's journey, keeping me interested, balanced, and at peace within myself, it would it be my interest in:

   a. concepts and learning.

   b. power and expressing my will.

   c. friendliness and cooperation.

   d. safety and security.

Indicate your total for each of the four options.

a _____ b _____ c _____ d _____

If most of your answers are:

- a: your preference is AIR-Dreamer-Mental
- b: your preference is FIRE-Realist-Social-Mental
- c: your preference is WATER-Catalyst-Social-Physical
- d: your preference is EARTH/Critic/Physical

My preference is: _____

In my case, I rated:

a ___23___ b ___7___ c ___46___ d ___14___

This indicates a preference for WATER-Catalyst-Social-Physical.

My partner rated:

a ___21___ b ___11___ c ___11___ d ___47___

His preference is EARTH-Critic-Physical.

Now that we have a clearer sense of our element preference, let's look at some additional ways to create awareness, increase our choices, and establish or maintain balance in our lives.

CHAPTER **2**

FRAMEWORKS FOR A BALANCED LIFE

We consistently seek to bring balance to our lives. Self-awareness is critical to start the journey, and a focused approached and understanding of where our psychological tension originates is critical to "work the process" along the way.

A good coach is someone who helps you to stay focused, set a specific goal or target, and move toward that goal or target in a systematic way. You can be your own coach, or you can ask a friend or colleague or your boss to serve as a coach for you.

Generating clear goals, using clear frameworks, and asking good questions are essential to good coaching results. A key to maintaining a personal balancing act is to understand that the coachee should develop only one new skill, goal, or outcome at a time.

The following two frameworks will assist the coachee in creating and getting clarity on a goal. One framework, called a problem-solving framework, uses timelines and phases. The other framework refers to the yoga chakra system, which helps in identifying imbalances in the body. These imbalances relate to unsatisfied personal needs and create an inner tension in order to gain our attention and help us in identifying a goal to fulfill, reduce the tension within, and bring us back to a balanced state.

Creating a clear goal based on processes identified in these two frameworks can assist the professional in staying balanced and working toward a balanced life.

We begin our coaching session by creating a clear goal based on what are often referred to as SMART criteria: The coachee identifies a goal that is S – specific, M – measurable, A – achievable, R – relevant, and T – timed. For example, if I say that I want to lose twenty pounds and I want to coach myself to achieve this, my goal statement would read something like this:

I will have reduced my weight by twenty pounds (specific, measurable), *which will make me feel healthier and more attractive* (relevant), *by December 31st of this year* (timed).

Maxwell Maltz, author of *Psycho-Cybernetics*,[2] said that human beings are goal-oriented organisms. An idea in our mind, activated in our mental awareness, stimulates us to make decisions and take action. As we move toward our goals, we are in a process of change.

Change can cause stress. An understanding of the following elemental personality problem-solving tools can help to reduce the impact of this stress and help us to reach our targeted outcome. It is important while journeying toward an outcome that you consider incoming feedback. As the journey affects you, it will create a need for you to reshape or reassess your desired outcome.

---

2   Maltz, Maxwell. *Psycho-Cybernetics*. Mass Market Paperbook. 1987.

QUESTIONING SKILLS AND THE
PROBLEM-SOLVING FRAMEWORK

Coaching skills rely heavily on the ability to ask good questions. The mind loves to solve problems, and by posing good questions to the mind, the mind can explore creative possibilities

We begin problem-solving by defining a current problem. A problem is the gap between your current reality and your desired outcome or goal. It is important to find ways to sort the problem so the problem is manageable and workable. We can sort for clarity by using timelines and posing questions.

TIMELINES. You can gain in-depth understanding of a problem if you look at it from the perspectives of past, present, and future. For example, if you want to lose weight but are struggling with the process, then review the desired outcome by flushing out distinctions from the different perspectives. Try to place yourself in the mindset for each perspective.

- **Past:** Start with the past. *In the past, what was the ideal weight for you? If it was 118 pounds and you now weigh 138 pounds, what made the difference? When did your weight change and what were your patterns that created the change? How far back in the past did this change take place? What was the driving reason behind the change?*
- **Present:** Now, take a look at the weight change from a present-tense perspective. *What is causing you to stay at this weight that you do not want? What would you now have to do differently to help you get back to your desired weight?*
- **Future:** Next, look at the weight problem from a future perspective. *Now that you weigh 118 pounds again, what did you do to get back to this desired weight? What will help you to*

maintain your desired outcome and keep off the twenty pounds? What will you have to do more of? Less of? Are you prepared to do that?

By asking timeline questions, you can sort out internal data that has always been available to you, but which you have not methodically and consciously thought through before and did not access.

When working to sort through a problem and set a goal, it is useful to use masking tape on the floor to create three boxes representing the past, the present, and the future. With each perspective, step into the appropriate box. This helps trigger the mind to come up with information to explore.

When we sort through data to review a problem, we study the cognitive structures of the experience. This allows us to see our process without the feelings of failure. The concept of failure has to do with the beliefs we hold about our ability. In this process, as in life, there is no failure, only feedback.

It is important to get to the root of a problem to understand fully all the associated issues. For example, we may ask, *"What stops you from achieving the goal weight of 118 pounds?"* Your answer might be, *"The fun and pleasure of the food and drink at the immediate moment takes over from my future dream of an ideal weight."*

The present is more immediate fun than the idea of a future abstract outcome. Now we are getting closer to the source of the problem. This information expands the problem area and we need to ask more questions, such as, *"What is fun and pleasurable in the immediate moment versus the future desire or outcome?"* The answer might be, *"When I'm with people who love to eat and drink, I am stimulated to eat and drink with them. In order for me to eat and drink less, I would have to be with people who are eating and drinking less."*

These questions and answers provide insight into how we relate to the challenge of achieving our future outcome. If the people around us stimulate us, then the problem is not just the eating patterns but also the association with others and our need to stay connected with them in a stimulating way.

This is an example of using feedback to sort out the experience of the problem and become more conscious of associated issues that influence the situation keeping us stuck. Since a problem is the gap between the current reality and the desired outcome or goal, the problem creates a feeling of tension within us. This tension to achieve the goal motivates us to continue to search for ways to eliminate the problem so the tension will go away. When striving to achieve our goals, we need to look for evidence that we are moving toward our outcome. The evidence needs to be tangible and reliable, which means it must be sensate-based. Someone else should be able to see it, touch it, smell it, hear it, or taste it.

Problem-solving processes appear to fail if we have not explored deeply enough into the problem. To look further requires more questions. For example, we might ask, *"What would be in the way of achieving the outcome you are after? Who else might be affected by your goal? How will they be affected?"* The answer might be, *"My husband enjoys eating and drinking, and we often reward ourselves with food and drink. Also, when we are stressed, we comfort ourselves by going out for a nice dinner. We would have to seriously change our patterns if I want to weigh less."*

It appears that the problem area of food and drink provides a strong emotional connection to people, especially to the husband. In order to get closer to the goal, new resources are needed. A resource is something that is not currently used but could be employed to help move from the present reality to the future goal.

We could ask, *"What resources would assist you in achieving your weight-loss goal?"* The answer might be, *"Drinking a low-calorie protein drink when hungry to avoid eating fat-producing foods and getting more exercise on a regular basis."*

These steps to problem-solving help us to gain a deeper understanding of the problem and the issues that can block achievement of the desired outcome or goal. We can see the whole process as different phases. In his book *Skills for the Future*,[3] Robert Dilts suggests using a movie technique called storyboarding for problem-solving. A storyboard builds a story one phase at a time. The phases used here to find our solutions and achieve our outcomes draw on the four elements.

PHASE 1: FIRST STORYBOARD
IDEA – DREAMER – AIR

Phase 1 draws on the mental awareness and the element of AIR. AIR provides us with insight and allows us to see new ideas. Because AIR is spacious, light, and everywhere, it is unencumbered by details and feelings. It is also not interested in the actions required to fulfill its own ideas. As AIR is intangible, it is unobstructed by the physical and social worlds of FIRE, WATER, and EARTH. For AIR to initiate images or visions, it has to be able to see new things. New things do not have physicality, memory, or emotional feelings attached to them from the past. New things look for generalities, or overviews, and are future-driven because they have not existed before or need to be re-created anew.

Phase 1: First Storyboard defines the future outcome, goal, or dream. For example: *In the future, I weigh 118 pounds.*

---

3   Dilts, Robert. *Skills for the Future*. California: Meta Publications. 1993.

PHASE 2: SECOND STORYBOARD
ACTION – REALIST – FIRE

FIRE comes into play next. It wants to connect the new idea to reality and take action. FIRE assumes the idea is possible and begins a trial-and-error process to move the idea forward by connecting actions to the idea, confronting and addressing anything that is in its current reality at the time.

Similar to the AIR element, FIRE is not that interested in cumbersome details or getting caught up in emotions that could slow the process. It is also not that interested in the actual building of the idea. Instead, it focuses on moving the idea forward and generates the heat or friction necessary to begin its realization. FIRE gets us involved by stimulating our energy and motivating us.

The FIRE element, with its outward and upward movements, holds onto the original vision (AIR), reminding us of the reason behind our actions, and maintains our focus on the immediate steps ahead. Moving the idea forward, FIRE adjusts its actions as it confronts new problems, continuously generating heat and friction along the way. Solution-driven, FIRE is present-focused as it looks for immediate things to do to bring the ideas of the Dreamer forward.

Phase 2: Second Storyboard creates realistic action items such as: *I will take a protein drink to maintain my blood-sugar levels and reduce feelings of hunger. I also will exercise on a regular basis.*

PHASE 3: THIRD STORYBOARD
REACTION – CATALYST – WATER

Next, the WATER element comes in and says, *"Wait a minute! You are not considering the impact of these actions on others. I don't feel right about the process or how quickly the steps are being taken."* This said, WATER then proceeds to do a consensus-check with everyone involved. *"How do you feel about this?"* Checking out the process driven by FIRE, WATER gathers data about how people are reacting to the process and to the idea in general.

This inquiry can often be challenging for WATER. As it questions the validity of AIR's idea and confronts the heat generated by FIRE's forward movement, WATER may also feel guilty about questioning and offending AIR and FIRE, but it wants to ensure social justice for all. WATER also is concerned that others may interpret its questioning as gossiping.

Phase 3: Third Storyboard deals with doubts and concerns involved in achieving the future goal using the actions established and asks, *"What about my husband and our tête-à-têtes? Will this change our relationship? How will we create new patterns and how will he feel about this."* Of course, WATER goes to friends to get their opinions, most likely before she discusses this with her husband. Drawing on the past, the future, and the present, WATER strives to "connect all the dots" and find a resolution to the needs of all involved.

When ideas (AIR), actions (FIRE), and reactions (WATER) mix with practical matter (EARTH), things can look muddled. WATER tries to blend the ideas and the actions from above downward to EARTH. It does this to assist in the manifestation of the idea of AIR and to slow the speed and reduce the friction generated by FIRE. This helps to stop things from burning up or burning out before the results are evident and the idea is in a tangible form. By slowing the process down, assimilation of the idea into practical matter begins to take shape.

PHASE 4: FOURTH STORY BOARD
MANIFESTATION – CRITIC – EARTH

The EARTH element, more focused on the wisdoms of past experiences, ensures a methodical and orderly process and brings together the ideas, the actions, and the reactions of the other phases by applying its thorough attention to details and understanding of the limitations involved in manifesting ideas. Now, we have a tangible form! Something now exists and can be touched, viewed, heard, tasted, smelled. The real physical world is evidenced and the idea is now not just a good idea with no substance. Through the social connectors (FIRE and WATER), ideas (AIR) begin to develop substance (EARTH). This holistic system assists us in developing a purposeful and conscious life. The natural elements of AIR, FIRE, WATER, and EARTH are the tools available for us to use to shape a life of meaning and purpose.

When presented with situations that place significant demands on us and pressure us to make decisions about who we really are, we realize that every decision we make affects us. As we make decisions, especially around serious situations, these decisions determine the course our lives take, thus shaping our character and personality along the way. When AIR, FIRE, WATER, and EARTH are well developed and maturely and consciously used, we have the makings of a well-tempered life.

Phase 4 completes the system, and our storyboards now look like this:

THE WHOLE SYSTEM AT WORK:
GETTING THE JOB DONE BY, WITH, AND THROUGH
PEOPLE

FIRST STORYBOARD: IDEA – Inspiration

SECOND STORYBOARD: ACTION – Process

THIRD STORYBOARD: REACTION – Process

FOURTH STORYBOARD: MANIFESTATION – Form

THE YOGA CHAKRA FRAMEWORK FOR IDENTIFYING TENSIONS AND UNSATISFIED NEEDS

Yoga provides a safe approach for integrating mind-body patterns that are used for balancing life's energies and promoting personal and spiritual growth. There are many benefits to practicing yoga. Some people say they feel relaxed, refreshed, vital, and stronger in the mind-body connection and healthier in the muscular-skeletal structure after performing yoga postures and breathing techniques. But yoga can provide us with more than just physical activities. Yoga also provides us with a complete and ancient system for understanding life.

The word "yoga" is derived from *yuj*, which means to bind together or yoke. Yoga binds the mind, body, and breath within the context of peace and bliss. The benefit is to enliven the expressions of coherency, congruency, and peacefulness within us.

Yoga is an ancient holistic system. It recognizes the body as an organism that is part of the cosmos and not separate from it. The ancient wise people saw the body as composed of the elements of AIR, FIRE, WATER, EARTH, and ETHER. They devised a yoga chakra system to describe the attributes of these elements. The word "chakra" means "wheel," and the chakra system decribes wheels or centers of consciousness that are related metaphysically to various parts of the spinal nerves. These centers of consciousness provide expressions of energy. When developed by the follower of yoga, they keep the mind-body system balanced and flowing.

Postures called "hatha" yoga and breathing exercises called "pranayamas" stimulate the spinal pathways and the chakra system. There are many chakras in the body, but most yoga teachings refer to seven, each dealing with an aspect of the human instrument and its development. These seven chakras are:

- **7th Chakra:** Sahasrara. Located at the crown, or the top of the head, this chakra deals with our intellect and its connection to the cosmos.
- **6th Chakra:** Ajna. Located at the forehead between the eyebrows, this chakra deals with our conscience and our ability to concentrate.
- **5th Chakra:** Vishuddha. Located at the throat, this chakra deals with our verbal expressions as well as our ability to take in air, water, food, and ideas.
- **4th Chakra:** Anahata. Located at the heart, this chakra provides a metaphysical link to the 5th chakra and to the lower chakras. It helps to purify the inner atmosphere with the outer atmosphere, and deals with our ability to develop tolerance and compassion as we maintain objective involvement with the world.
- **3rd Chakra:** Manipura. Located at the region of the solar plexus, this chakra deals with our will and our sense of power. It also deals with how we take our ideas out into the world and how effectively we confront the challenges we meet along the way.
- **2nd Chakra:** Svadisthana. Located at the area of the lower abdomen, this chakra is associated with reproduction, cooperation, and affiliation and how we mix energies with others.
- **1st Chakra:** Muladhara. Located at the base of the spine, this chakra deals with our ability to bind materials together, manifest tangible results, and address how secure we feel in the world around us.

TWO DRIVING FORCES

Yoga uses two fundamental driving forces to relate our basic human needs to the chakra energy centers. One force attends to our "being," or spiritual side, and the other focuses on the "human," or worldly side.

The "being" side is concerned with unconditional love, faith, and the use of prayer and meditation. These approaches tap into a belief system that supports seeing ourselves not just as individuals, but also as individuals connected to the whole universe. The three upper chakras relate to the spiritual side.

The "human" side of ourselves is conditional and bases much of its decision-making processes on the fear instinct and the tension of opposite functions. If there is good, there is also bad. If there is light, there is also darkness. If there is a limited supply, then there is competition. The four lower chakras relate to the human side, and the link between "human" and "being" is through the fourth chakra, Anahata, located at the heart. In a metaphorical sense, this could be called the "Christ" center, the link between above and below, between heaven and Earth.

The fourth chakra is where the teachings of forgiveness, peace, and compassion are expressed, tools that can bridge the gap between one human being and another human being. If we are immature, we strive to satisfy our needs at the expense of another human being. If we are mature, we strive to maintain harmony, balance, and constructive connections with others. Bridging the gap between self and others in appropriate ways can provide opportunities for us to learn, grow, and evolve. We realize more than ever that we are totally interconnected and interdependent on each other for life on planet Earth. In society, just as within ourselves, when one part of the system is weak and imbalanced, it throws the whole system off balance.

When negative stress is evident in the human system, it manifests as imbalances in one or more parts of the body and affects one or more of the seven chakras, or centers of consciousness.

When we are in the grips of the four lower chakras, we tend to see things from an inherent fear response of "fight or flight." This response was necessary for our survival when we lived in life-threatening situations. Although we are now "civilized," we still often experience perceived danger when we interact with others.

This perceived danger triggers our fear response and sends biochemical releases, such as adrenalin, throughout the body. If the energy of these biochemicals builds up without appropriate release, it creates imbalances within us that manifest in weakening and breaking down our system. We may lose sleep, develop ulcers, become angry or impatient with others, get headaches, or develop some other form of expression of imbalance that needs attention.

If we do not attend to an imbalance, it will become worse and can lead to serious consequences—even death. It is best if we can become aware of and consciously see a problem and address an imbalance and coach our way back to a balanced state before our health is diminished. Using the chakra system to identify imbalances, we can work to correct them.

THE YOGA CHAKRA SYSTEM

CHAKRA	CHARACTERISTICS	BALANCED	IMBALANCED
7th: SAHASRARA	Location: Crown of head Color: Magenta Element: Space Function: Fine intellect	Meditative Calmness Clarity	Stress Insomnia Anxiety

6th: AJNA	Location: Forehead Color: Purple Element: Energy Function: Consciousness	Concentration	Poor concentration Loss of equilibrium
5th: VISHUDDHA	Location: Throat Color: Blue Element: Ether Function: Purity	Purification of expressions	Poor facilitation of breath
4th: ANAHATA	Location: Chest Color: Green Element: AIR Function: Understanding; courage; compassion; humility; self-actualization	Mixture of outer and inner atmospheres for warmth and calmness	Worry Congestion Cowardliness
3rd: MANIPURA	Location: Solar plexus Color: Yellow Element: FIRE Function: Emotional force; willpower	Churning of inner refinement processes	Irritability Poor metabolism Poor digestion
2nd: SVADISTHANA	Location: Lower abdomen, reproductive Color: Orange Element: WATER Function: Emotional reactions; harmony; affiliation	Blending of all elements	Martyrdom Poor circulation Poor relationships
1st: MULADHARA	Location: Coccyx sacral Color: Red Element: EARTH Function: Security; shelter; survival	Binding of all elements Foundation Stability	Fearfulness Skeletal-muscular problems

We can see that the yoga chakra system provides a good understanding of our processes and that yoga is more than just a physical system of postures. It is also a spiritual process of self-understanding. It can be seen as a holistic system that provides an understanding of ourselves as part of nature and the cosmos. Using yoga physical poses and practices, however, can provide us with an effective approach to balance our elements and develop coherence of the mind-body connection.

Here are a few suggestions to help you in your practice of yoga at home:

ENVIRONMENT. Create an environment that allows you to withdraw from the outer world. If possible, set aside a separate room or a part of a room for your practice. Include in this space incense for the sense of smell, beautiful pictures for the sense of sight, and artifacts, images, or symbols that give you inspiration and enjoyment. The environment should stimulate joy, happiness, and bliss.

POSTURES. Many people think of yoga as hatha yoga: performing physical postures. These postures assist the mind and body in releasing tension and creating relaxation. Hatha yoga teachers suggest holding each posture for ten to thirty seconds to create a static stretch.

There are four basic postures that are designed to re-energize the body. They consist of:

Forward bend   Backward bend

Inverted pose   Twisting pose

Most of the poses used in a typical yoga class will be a variation of these four movements. Of course, we do not want to forget the resting pose at the end of a yoga session. The resting pose allows the body to register the effects of the previous poses.

Yoga postures and practices provide the opportunity for us to step back and take a break from the world. Doing a regular routine allows us to stretch out the tension in the muscles, relax the mind, and let go of life's cares. In addition, we benefit from developing strength and flexibility, improving coordination, and increasing cardiovascular efficiency.

Following are examples of these four basic postures you might like to try:

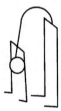

Forward bends

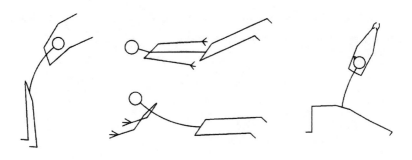

Backward bends

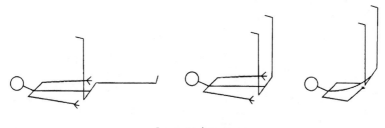

Inverted poses

Twisting poses

Another excellent series of spinal movements is performed through the Sun Salutation. This quick and easy way to stimulate the spinal chakras is performed as follows:

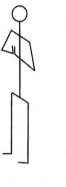

1. Stand erect, feet together, exhale, and bring your hands into a prayer position with forearms parallel to the floor.

2. Inhale and arch backward until your arms are stretched overhead, hips forward, head, shoulders and neck relaxed.

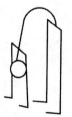

3. Exhale and bend forward, palms toward the floor, head to legs—feel free to bend your knees so you are not putting an uncomfortable strain on your lower back.

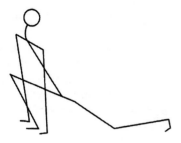

4. Inhale and thrust your right leg back, touching the floor with the knee, fingertips in line with the left toes, palms on the floor. Move your hips downward toward the floor, left knee bent (do not go beyond the toes to avoid strain), arch backward, and look up.

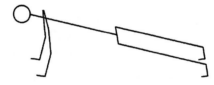

5. Hold your breath and go into a pushup position, neck and spine in a straight line, feet together, and arms straight.

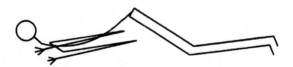

6. Exhale and bring your knees, chest, and chin to the floor, keeping elbows bent and close to the body.

7. Inhale and glide forward with your chest lifted slightly off the floor, arching backward, elbows slightly bent, pelvis down, legs outstretched, and look up.

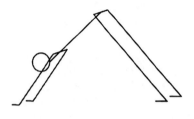

8. Exhale, curl your toes under, lift your buttocks upward to create a triangle position with your tailbone toward the ceiling, and press your heels to the floor, head and shoulders hanging downward between the arms.

9. Inhale and bring the right foot forward between your hands, left knee down, and look up, as in pose 4.

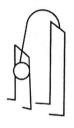

10. Exhale and bring your feet together, head to legs, as in pose 3.

11. Inhale and stretch up, then bend backward with arms overhead as in pose 2.

12. Exhale and return to pose 1.

Now, breathe deeply. This completes half a round. To complete the full round, go through the series again, working with the left leg in pose 4 and pose 9. At the end of the series, breathe deeply.

After two complete rounds, stand still for a moment. Feel the flow of energy from the increased circulation. Feel recharged and revitalized, then lie in the resting pose to relax for a couple of minutes.

BREATHING. Breathing techniques, or pranayamas, as they are called in yoga, help calm the mind and purify energy channels in the body. They include:

- **Complete breath.** Inhale through the nose, filling the lungs and stomach with air. Hold the breath for a second or two, then exhale slowly through the mouth, pushing out all the air. Perform this breath five to ten times.
- **Alternate-nostril breath.** Close the right nostril with your right thumb. Place your right index and middle fingers on your forehead between the eyebrows. (These two fingers between the eyebrows are to remind you that you are more than the body and the mind. Holding this point between the eyebrows stimulates the Ajna chakra of conscience and concentration.)

Inhale through the left nostril, then close the left nostril with your right ring finger. Hold the breath for a second or two, then release your thumb and exhale through the right nostril. Pause for a second or two, then inhale through the right nostril, close both nostrils and hold the breath, and then release your ring finger and exhale through the left nostril. Continue this pattern for a minute or two.

MEDITATION. Meditation, or sitting in silence, is performed by focusing your mind on your breath or on some sound such as "om" that you silently repeat. The yogis say that the "om" sound incorporates all sounds and has a complete vibration. This approach of focusing on your breath or on a sound provides the mind with a focus. The mind needs a focus in order for it to become still and to stop its jumping from thought to thought.

Gently introduce the breath or sound and allow the mind to focus on it in a gentle manner. The mind may still wander. Once you recognize that this has happened, gently reintroduce the breath or sound.

Do this process for five to twenty minutes, then slowly bring your attention back to the room, then back to your body. Lie down in resting pose for a few minutes before going into activity. This rest will allow the nervous system to register the effects meditation has had on the mind-body and is an important part of meditation.

Practice these suggestions on a regular basis to rest and repair physical tensions created from everyday life. In doing this, you will strengthen your nervous system and its ability to deal with demands and pressures. Regular retreats from the hectic world will fortify your ability to adapt and cope, bringing about an accumulative relaxation response that refreshes the nervous system and counters the effects of stress. To feel the full benefits, perform these activities once or twice every day.

NOTE: *If you have a medical concern such as high blood pressure or have not been engaged in exercise for some time, get your doctor's permission before doing any of the above procedures. If you have high blood pressure, go gently into the inverted poses or avoid them altogether so that you are not putting additional pressure on your heart. Do not perform any poses within your first three months of pregnancy. Do not engage in poses directly after eating heavy meals. The body spends a great deal of energy during digestion and this will distract the mind-body as well as make the practice of yoga physically uncomfortable.*

DEVELOPING AWARENESS THROUGH YOGA AND THE CHAKRA SYSTEM

By using our understanding of the four lower chakras, we get a map to health, wellness, happiness, and balance. The four lower chakras relate more to the physical body and the ego-driven personality. They provide the insight and tools needed to create a well-tempered life.

The enlightened use of these tools assists us in satisfying our human need for living a full and happy life. They also pave the way for increased spirituality by strengthening our connection to the upper three chakras. When we are pulled down into the struggles of the lower chakras without conscious awareness of the issues we are dealing with, we tend to be stuck in the negative use of the elemental expressions. In this state, we are often unable to consider higher, more spiritual expressions of ourselves.

Industrial psychologist Abraham Maslow used a hierarchy of needs to demonstrate a similar point.[4] He stated that until each lower need

---

4   Maslow, Abraham. *Toward a Psychology of Being.* Third Edition. New York: Wiley. 1998.

on the hierarchy was met, we cannot move up to the next need. We can apply his theory to the chakra system.

If the Muladhara chakra, the security need, is not satisfied, we will continue to struggle to build a world that we feel safe to live in. Once our security needs are fulfilled, the next need is to find someone to share our life. This need is connected to the motivation to affiliate with others and is similar to the Svadhisthana chakra, which is above the Muladhara or base chakra.

After the need for affiliation is satisfied, we then strive to move to the next need, which deals with our will or sense of personal power. At this chakra, we move from being dependent on the structures and rules of the land and people to feeling independent, and we now want recognition for our uniqueness. This need is closely associated with the Manipura chakra's energy expression, or the force of our personal will and how we use that force in the world with others. For example: Do we take and grab while expressing our will? Or do we fight injustices by confronting and dealing with issues in a mature and respectful way while honoring self and others?

The fourth chakra, Anahata, deals with our need to learn, grow, and understand. Without compassion, we lose our sense of interdependency that links us to the preservation of human life. Once compassion toward self and others is developed and expressed, we become more consciously and consistently linked to the three upper chakras related to our being, or spiritual side.

This yoga chakra system helps us to understand how we can strengthen the link of the human being of the physical world with the human being of the spiritual world.

For a well-tempered life, we can focus on developing the more mature use of the tools to develop and strengthen our connection to our higher, more spiritual expressions. In the four lower chakras, we find the tools to help us navigate our journey through life. As we become more aware of how the tools are used, we link more consciously to the upper three chakras. This developmental process takes place throughout our lives.

The first set of tools, then, has to do with developing our self-awareness. The next sets of tools take us into developing a focused approach to goal-setting and an understanding of where our imbalances originate. Now that we have identified and clarified what these imbalances might be, we can see how they affect us and provide some suggestions to reestablish balance.

CHAPTER 3

COACHING FOR
HEALTH AND WELLNESS

We have discussed how to use the problem-solving framework and the yoga chakra framework as systems for identifying and clarifying imbalances in the body, mind, and spirit. The problem-solving framework draws on Western approaches of a cognitive style. The yoga chakra framework draws on Eastern approaches and speaks more to physiology, to energy imbalances and how to balance the system by understanding our *doshas*—what we relate and refer to in this book as elements.

Connecting these Western and Eastern approaches together, we can link the AIR element to the Vata dosha, the FIRE and WATER elements to the Pitta dosha, and the EARTH element to the Kapha dosha. Let's now take a look at the ties between elements and doshas, and what the recommendation might be to bring each element/dosha into balance, or, for some of us, to continue to maintain balance in that element/dosha.

PERSONALITY PATTERNS: ATTRIBUTES RELATED TO ELEMENT EXPRESSIONS			
AIR	**FIRE**	**WATER**	**EARTH**
Mental	Social-mental	Social-physical	Physical
Dreamer	Realist	Catalyst	Critic
Vata	Pitta	Pitta	Kapha
Emphasis: Ideas and concepts; vision	Emphasis: Actions; moving ideas forward	Emphasis: Emotional reactions	Emphasis: Final product or outcome
BALANCED			
Provides overviews and improves systems	Leads others and others follow	Makes links; tries to "connect the dots"	Detail-oriented
Single-minded focus	Quick and forceful	Empathetic	Patient
Offers ideas for sake of ideas; happy to leave details to others	Works in trial-and-error ways seeking next solution	Flexible; can jump from one action item to another	Systematic; plodding
Works independently; stimulated by ideas	Great delegator when moving projects forward	Multi-tasker	Methodical
Draws on future possibilities and improvements	Draws on present, focusing quickly on next set of action items	Draws on past, present, and future to tend to whole picture	Draws on past

Generates new ideas, inventions, systems	Connects ideas to next immediate actions	Connects others together	Works for others
Spends eagerly on ideas and investments believed in	Spends what needs to be spent to get job done	Gives money freely to others	Good at saving money and generating wealth
IMBALANCED			
Distant and aloof	Dominating	Murky or vague; lacking focus or clarity	Stubborn and stuck
Abstract	Overpowering	Confusing to others	Judgmental
Low tolerance for disturbances	Too fast – misses nuances	Too scattered	Too slow
Not interested in people's emotions	Steps on toes	Lacks boundaries	Closed-minded
Misunderstood; may be abandoned by others	Insensitive, may be avoided by others	Martyred; can be mistreated by others	Longstanding suffering due to feeling taken for granted by others
Short-sighted; sees money only as resource to satisfy next idea	Spends, takes, and forgets to replenish	Overly generous; forgets self in equation	Hoarding for sake of hoarding

We need to be more conscious of the areas of our body that are physically affected by life's demands and pressures. Imbalances can come from many stresses and strains of life. Different situations may cause stress or tension to appear in different places. For example, we may get headaches when we are overstressed at work, but back problems when we are under financial stress.

Identifying the areas of your physical reactions to the demands and pressures in your life is important to understand how to counteract the negative stressors. We can strengthen the physically exhausted or weak areas through various wellness techniques.

WHERE DOES STRESS APPEAR IN YOUR BODY?

Refer to the following checklist of stress symptoms, which are grouped into three categories of A, B, and C. First, identify the typical stress symptoms that you have had over the course of your life when you have been under serious stress or had many demands and pressures placed on you. Next, analyze the stresses and strains that are affecting you right now. Review both ratings and see which element/dosha shows typical imbalances, then look at the recommendations of what you can do to bring it back into balance.

By reviewing this checklist, we can start to see our patterns of physical stress. We then can take the necessary steps to alleviate the pressure on that part of our body. Rate yourself on the symptoms of each category on a scale of 1 (almost never) to 5 (very often). Total your ratings for each category and review where you are most imbalanced.

STRESS SYMPTOMS CHECKLIST

A symptoms	1	2	3	4	5
Forgetful					
Easily distracted					
Constipated					
Light, interrupted sleep					

Mood swings					
Restlessness					
Confusion					
Headaches					
Dry skin					
B symptoms	1	2	3	4	5
Quick-tempered					
High blood pressure					
Scattered					
Impatient					
Activity overloaded					
Excessive body heat					
Sensitive skin					
Intolerance of hot weather					
Stomach aches					
C symptoms	1	2	3	4	5
Dullness					
Slowness					
Depressed					
Gain weight					
Judgmental					
Oily skin					
Possessive					
Bone or muscle aches					
Lack of energy					

Place your total for each category of symptoms in the space provided to find out which function currently is most imbalanced for you.

A symptoms _____ /45
B symptoms _____ /45
C symptoms _____ /45

A total for a category of symptoms greater than 31 would indicate a high level of imbalance and the need for immediate attention to this function. A total for a category of 16 to 30 would indicate a moderate level of imbalance and the need for some attention to this function. A total of 15 or less would indicate a low level of imbalance, or an acceptable level of balance.

For example, let's consider the case where the totals are 30 for A symptoms, 18 for B symptoms, and 25 for C symptoms. This would indicate the need to attend first to A, Vata Mental-Dreamer-AIR, which is most imbalanced, then to C, Kapha Physical-Critic-EARTH. The total is lowest for B, Pitta Social-Realist/Catalyst-FIRE/WATER, indicating it is least imbalanced.

A. Deals with our mental function and governs motion: flow of endocrine and nerve impulses, for example. In yoga, we refer to this principle as Vata. Vata is fast, cold and dry by nature. These qualities increase during fall and winter, the Vata season.

B. Deals with our social function and governs energy production: metabolism, digestion, and elimination. In yoga, we refer to this principle as Pitta. Pitta is hot and intense by nature. These qualities increase in summer, the Pitta season.

C. Deals with our physical function and governs structure and physical balance: formation of muscles, fat, bone, and sinew. In yoga, we refer to this principle as Kapha. Kapha is slow, cold, and wet by nature. These qualities increase in spring, the Kapha season.

- When Vata is balanced, the mental processes are experienced as alert, imaginative, sensitive, spontaneous, resilient, and exhilarated.

- To balance the Vata Mental-Dreamer-AIR in you, you need to calm your system with regular routine. You can do this by going to bed early, eating meals at the same time every day, having regular elimination, keeping warm in cold weather, drinking plenty of warm liquids, and avoiding stimulants.

- When Pitta is balanced, the social processes are experienced as confident, intellectual, enterprising, and joyous.

- To balance the Pitta Social-Realist/Catalyst-FIRE/WATER in you, you need to cool your emotions and use moderation to bring your system back into balance. You can do this by avoiding excessive exposure to heat and sun, abstaining from alcohol and tobacco, easing up on tight deadlines and excessive levels of activities, and not skipping meals.

- When Kapha is balanced, the physical processes are experienced as strong, calm, enduring, and caring.

- To balance the Kapha Physical-Critic-EARTH in you, you need to give the body more stimulation to overcome feeling heavy, lethargic, and dull. You can do this by avoiding excessive rest and oversleeping, reducing intake of sweets, getting plenty of exercise, keeping warm in cold, wet weather, and seeking out greater variety in life.

REFLEXOLOGY TO IMPROVE BALANCE

As well as yoga postures and techniques to bring the system back into balance, we can also draw on the ancient art of reflexology. Reflexology is a safe and simple technique for stimulating and balancing the personality elements. This is done by working on the reflexes of the ears, hands, and feet that relate to our body parts and systems. Through the application of deep compression massage and pressure point work, circulation is increased to the corresponding body reflexes. This improved circulation stimulates and assists in balancing the elements.

EAR REFLEXOLOGY:
CALMING THE MENTAL FUNCTION

To bring balance to the AIR processes and calm the mental function, we can apply pressure point work to our ears, thereby stimulating the entire body system through the reflexes in the ear. Imagine the ear as an inverted fetus.

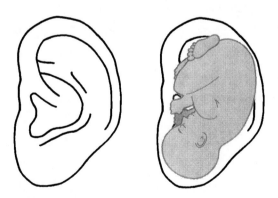

The head reflexes, for example, are worked when you apply pressure to the earlobe.

Ear Reflexes

The following diagram describes how to view the location of reflex points in the ear and the corresponding body systems.

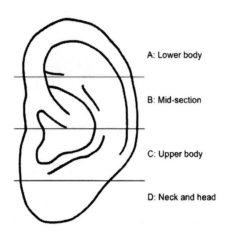

A. The upper part of the ear corresponds to the lower body. Applying pressure here stimulates reflexes in the legs, hips, thighs, reproductive organs, knees, part of the urinary system, and hands and arms.

B. The middle part of the ear corresponds to the mid-section of the body. Applying pressure here stimulates reflexes in the intestines, stomach, liver, spleen, gall bladder, and part of the urinary system.

C. The mid-to-lower part of the ear corresponds to the upper body. Applying pressure here stimulates reflexes in the chest, breasts, lungs, upper neck, and back.

D. The lower part of the ear corresponds to the top of the body. Applying pressure here stimulates reflexes in the neck, head, and brain.

Ear Zones

The ear is also divided into three zones that relate to the body systems.

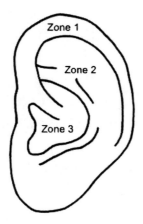

Zone 1: The outer area of the ear represents the excretory systems, such as the respiratory and digestive systems, as well as the circulatory system. Disorders are evidenced through abnormal redness (exceptions being color caused from vigorous exercise or cold temperature).

Zone 2: The middle area of the ear represents the nervous system as well as the skeletal system. Abnormal protrusion could indicate a persistent, self-imposing, stubborn nature. Abnormal redness in this area could indicate a nervous disorder.

Zone 3: The inner area of the ear represents the internal organs and processes such as the heart, colon, lungs, and stomach. Abnormal redness could be an indication of an imbalance.

EAR SELF-CHECKS

Healing arts specialists suggest that you check your own ears for the following:

- Tightness and tension could be an indication of stressful circumstances.
- Warm ears could indicate good circulation in the body.
- Skin peeling and white flakes on the ear could indicate toxic waste buildup in the body.
- Red spots or lines on the ears could indicate an acute situation in the body, perhaps an inflammation.
- If the flesh of the ears feels loose, this could indicate low energy due to illness or lack of vitality.
- Brownish skin tone on part of the ear could indicate poor circulation in that body reflex area.

BENEFITS OF EAR REFLEXOLOGY

When performing reflexology on the ears, a calming sensation is often felt throughout the body. Healing arts specialists think this effect occurs because the ears are close to the central nervous system.

When you feel disoriented, confused, or unclear (stress symptoms of imbalance in the AIR element), working the ears can help to calm and create a renewed sense of well-being.

HAND REFLEXOLOGY: COOLING THE SOCIAL FUNCTIONS

Hand Reflexes

The following diagram describes the location of reflex points in the hands and the corresponding body systems.

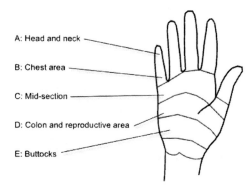

A: Head and neck
B: Chest area
C: Mid-section
D: Colon and reproductive area
E: Buttocks

A. When pressure is applied to the fingertips, the head and brain are reflexed. When pressure is applied along the length of the fingers, the neck is reflexed.

B. When pressure is applied to the upper part of the hand just under the fingers, the chest, breasts, lungs, and upper back areas are reflexed.

C. When pressure is applied to the middle part of the hand, the stomach, liver, spleen, gall bladder, pancreas, middle back, and kidneys are reflexed.

D. When pressure is applied to the lower part of the hand, the colon, reproductive system, and lower back areas are reflexed.

E. When pressure is applied to the base of the hand, the buttocks area is reflexed.

Hand Zones

The hands are also divided into five zones that relate to the body systems.

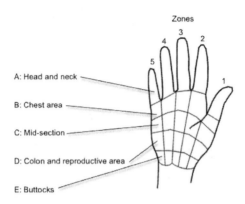

Zone 1: The thumb is the reflex area for the central nervous system, spinal column, and generally those reflex areas of the center of the body.

Zones 2 and 3: The index and middle fingers relate to the reflex points for areas of the body that include the eyes, neck, chest, stomach, colon, and lower back.

Zones 4 and 5: The ring and baby fingers are the reflex areas for the ears and peripheral areas of the body such as the shoulder blades, outer ribcage, hips, and ascending and descending colon.

HAND SELF-CHECKS

When working your hands, healing arts specialists suggest looking for the following:

- Warm hands could indicate good circulation in the body.
- Fingernails lined with vertical or horizontal grooves could indicate chronic stress.
- White spots on the nails could indicate trauma affecting the body. If the trauma is current, the spots will be close to the cuticle. If the trauma happened about three months ago, the spots will be midway up the nail. If the spots are near the tip of the nail, the trauma was approximately six months ago.

- Skin that feels loose could indicate low energy due to illness or lack of vitality.

BENEFITS OF HAND REFLEXOLOGY

Hand reflexology may produce a comforting feeling internally. When we are worried or upset, we tend to wring our hands. This is a healing response. Working the hands helps to cool the emotional state. Healing arts specialists think this effect could occur because the hands, linked by the arms, are connected to the chest cavity, which is the seat of the heart, or Anahata, center of consciousness in yoga.

When you feel angry, frustrated, lonely, or sad (stress symptoms of imbalance in the FIRE and the WATER elements), working the hands can help to cool distressing feelings.

FOOT REFLEXOLOGY: STIMULATING THE PHYSICAL FUNCTION

When reflexology is performed on the feet, two basic effects are experienced: feeling grounded and feeling energized. For example, if you are lethargic, depressed, or fatigued, working the feet can be physically stimulating for the body and can create a sense of feeling more "in your body."

Foot Reflexes

The diagram below describes the location of reflex points in the feet and the corresponding body systems.

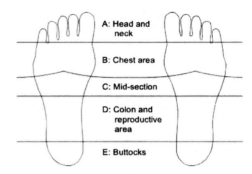

The toes correspond to the head and neck of the body. The brain is reflexed when pressure is applied to the tips of the toes. The neck is reflexed when pressure is applied along the length of the toes.

A. The ball of the foot is located from the base of the toes to the start of the instep and corresponds to the chest area of the body. The chest, breasts, lungs, and upper back are reflexed when pressure is applied to the ball of the foot.

B. The mid-section of the foot corresponds to the stomach, liver, spleen, gall bladder, pancreas, upper back, and kidneys. These areas are reflexed when pressure is applied to the part of the foot from just below the area of the "bunion" joint to just above where the foot structure narrows.

C. The lower part of the foot corresponds to the colon, reproductive system, and lower back. These areas are reflexed when pressure is applied to this area of the foot.

D. The heel of the foot corresponds to the lower back and buttocks. These areas are reflexed when pressure is applied to the heel.

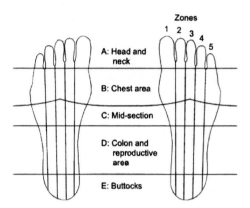

Foot Zones

The foot is also divided into five zones that relate to the body's systems.

Zone 1: The big toe is the reflex area for the central nervous system, spine, and body reflexes related to the center of the body.

Zones 2 and 3: The second and third toes are the reflex areas for the parts of the body slightly off the middle or center of the spine and cover parts of the reflexes for the eyes, neck, chest, stomach, colon, and lower back.

Zones 4 and 5: The fourth and fifth (baby) toes are the reflex areas for the ears and peripheral areas of the body such as the shoulder blades, outer ribcage, hips, and ascending and descending colon.

FOOT SELF-CHECKS

When working the feet, healing art specialists suggest looking for the following:

- Warm feet could indicate good circulation in the body.
- Toenails lined with vertical or horizontal grooves could indicate chronic stress.
- Cracked heels could indicate poor circulation in the lower buttocks and the possibility of hemorrhoids.
- Calluses on the balls of the feet could indicate a blockage in circulation around the chest, breast, and lung area.
- Swollen areas in the feet could indicate a pooling of waste products.
- Skin that feels loose could indicate low energy due to illness or lack of vitality.
- Tight skin could indicate a high level of stress and tension.
- Thin skin could be an indication of oversensitivity to others while thick skin could be an indication of a stubborn personality.

BENEFITS OF FOOT REFLEXOLOGY

Foot reflexology can produce feelings of being more grounded and more energetic. This grounded and energized effect is thought to occur because the feet connect us to the Earth.

When you feel disjointed, run down, or ungrounded (symptoms of imbalance in the EARTH element), working the feet can help to create a sense of balance and harmony.

MIND-BODY IMBALANCES IN MENTAL, SOCIAL, OR PHYSICAL AWARENESSES

Another way to look at imbalances of the mind-body is to consider the three fundamental processes that the body performs to keep us healthy and functioning properly: coordination and control, energy and waste, and standing and moving. These processes can be related to the mental, social-mental, social-physical, and physical awarenesses and the four elements of AIR, FIRE, WATER, and EARTH.

Coordination and control. Coordination and control relate to our mental awareness and the element of AIR. They are linked to our body in the following ways:

- The nervous system (AIR). This deals with how much we feel we are in control of living our vision and fulfilling our destiny.
- The endocrine system (AIR). This deals with how much we feel we are in control of coordinating the people and events in our life so that we can live our vision and fulfill our destiny.

When we have problems in the mind-body systems that deal with coordination and control, we could be experiencing challenges in how we are thinking about ourselves, our purpose, or our future prospects in life. To balance these challenges, it is useful to work the reflexes in the ears to calm the mind and regain clarity and direction.

Energy and waste removal. Energy and waste removal relate to our social awarenesses and the elements of FIRE and WATER. They are linked to our body in the following ways:

- The digestive system (FIRE). This deals with how we process incoming data and approach the world around us.
- The urinary system (FIRE and WATER). This deals with how we feel about and handle criticism.
- The respiratory and circulatory systems (WATER). This deals with how we feel about the flow of our life.

When we have problems in the mind-body systems that deal with energy and waste removal, we could be experiencing challenges in how we are assimilating and processing events and people around us. To balance these challenges, it is useful to work the reflexes in the hands to cool upsets and trigger healing releases.

Standing and moving. Standing and moving relate to our physical awareness and the element of EARTH. They are linked to our body in the following way:

- The bones, muscles, and ligaments (EARTH). These deal with how comfortable and safe we feel about the structures in our world and whether or not we feel supported.

When we have problems in our mind-body systems that deal with bones, muscles, and ligaments, we could be struggling with the structures that keep us upright or that make us feel tied down and burdened. We may be questioning if we are moving forward, stuck in the past, or standing still. To balance these challenges, it is useful to work the reflexes in the feet to stimulate changes while creating a sense of being centered, grounded, and energized.

REFLEXOLOGY IN GENERAL

Whether working the ears, hands, or feet, you will feel the circulation effect on the body, and this will tend to heighten relaxation. By stimulating the reflexes, circulation is improved and we feel the relaxation of tensions within, which promotes a balancing effect of the related body systems.

People in the healing arts, particularly Oriental health practitioners who look at the body with understanding of meridians and yin/yang energy, can offer additional insight into the complexities of the body and additional ways to understand and address our mental, social, physical, and spiritual wellness.

PART II

COACHING FOR A
WELL-TEMPERED LIFE

In this section, we will elaborate on coaching tools, the frameworks of problem-solving and the yoga chakra system, and build on our understanding of reflexology techniques in conjunction with the elements of AIR, FIRE, WATER, and EARTH and the development of the qualities and characteristics of a well-tempered life—a life that is shaped, refined, and honed to express its highest purpose.

*Tempered: possessing both the hardiness
and the flexibility needed to be resilient*

CHAPTER 4

THE AIR ELEMENT

When we work with the energies of the fourth chakra, Anahata, we are dealing with our identity, our purpose in life, our visions, and our dreams for the future. This fourth chakra expression is best described by the AIR element. Following is an example of a self-expression by an AIR-preferred person we will call "Richard" in response to a question during his coaching to gain greater self-awareness.

The question was: *How would you describe yourself, your strengths, and your gifts, and how you strive to share these with the world?*

WHAT IS AN AIR TYPE LIKE?

The AIR element relates to our mental awareness and manifests through our ideas and thoughts. Richard is a person who prefers the AIR element. He is always questioning why things cannot be different and why people find him difficult. In his words:

"I questioned everything and would ask, why? My mind could see things that other people could not. People often thought I was trying to cause problems. But I was just trying to show them how to expand their view.

"I was forever telling my mother how to dress. I would say, just add a little something here, or remove something there. I love beauty and elegance and can easily recognize it. I have a natural disdain for ugliness and squalor. I want to make people see that they can aspire to the finer things in life. I would go about telling people what to do and what not to do in order to challenge their current thinking.

"I could never understand why people didn't take to me as I was only trying to make a better world for all of us. I was never too interested in people's emotions; I think emotions are a waste of time. When people would get upset with me, I would scratch my head and wonder what was wrong with them.

"Over the years, I have tried to learn more about people's reactions and what makes them do the things they do. I am still not that comfortable with their personal issues. I am always thinking that we should be working on creating a beautiful world for everyone and not bother with other issues. I'm not afraid to tell people what I see. If they don't like it, well, what can I do? I'm trying to improve things. God knows others do not see what is needed.

"I'm not afraid to pour myself into projects, nor am I afraid to ruffle a few feathers in the process. But when people get bogged down with too many problems and my ideas don't seem to be coming to fruition, I can lose interest and move on to something a little more possible and challenging, or at least something with a little more interest to me.

"Sometimes I wonder if I am really meant for this world as I don't seem to fit in. Other people appear much more comfortable accepting things as they are. I often get strange looks from people. I used to think people looked at me this way because they respected me or envied me, but now I question

that. Perhaps they don't understand me at all. I am neither a snob, nor do I want to be different from others. It is just that I see things that they don't see.

"If people paid less attention to their personal needs, they would have a far better chance at creating a life that could contribute to future generations.

"My mission on this planet is to ensure that beauty and elegance are forever in the forefront of people's minds. We should never settle for less than near perfection, and even if I have to ruffle a few feathers to cause change to happen on this planet, I am prepared to do this. In fact, I must do this, for this is my purpose to ensure that something new and improved comes forth at all times."

HOW TO RECOGNIZE AND DEAL WITH PITFALLS OF THE AIR TYPE

Creative, focused attention is the gift of the AIR person. When taking the perspective of the AIR element without the tempering of the other elements, people can be seen as "things," or components within a system. This is a pitfall of the detached AIR element when it lacks the full development of the other three elements. For example, we can see this detachment of the social and physical sides in business when companies downsize. People are let go from their positions without concern for their personal lives. Another example of excluding the social and physical sides is when governments drop bombs on countries without regard for human life. They rationalize these activities in some way to justify them. When people are considered in a dehumanizing way, it is easier to treat them as components within a system.

Without compassion, we give little thought to the consequences people experience. We get bored with "people" stuff and find reasons not to get involved because we find their problems tedious and not worth our time. We concern ourselves with what we consider to be more important and justify any human cost by whatever rationale we use. It is difficult to be compassionate when the mental awareness is out of touch with social and physical distinctions.

If our preference for the mental awareness is without the development of the other awarenesses, we remain an imbalanced and immature expression of the whole of ourselves. Creating pie-in-the-sky ideas, we would flit from one enterprise to another and never materialize our ideas into anything useful. We would live a confusing egocentric life and deteriorate into the stern personality of an abandoned, lonely, one-dimensional, black-and-white person; but we would feel that, after all, we were right in our worldview.

Without a well-developed connection to the social parts of ourselves, we have difficulty manifesting something tangible from a visionary perspective. To process an idea, we need to interact more with others. If, for example, I come up with the idea for a business, the next step is to connect with people. I have to contact suppliers, potential clients, and bankers, accountants, and other professionals to help me pull together the business. In this way, I come out of the realm of the Dreamer and start to bring in the elements of FIRE, WATER, and EARTH.

By interfacing with the social aspects, I begin to make the idea more tangible. The social side and processes take longer than the mental side because to come up with an idea takes no time at all but to connect with others is time-consuming.

Even after lots of connections with people on the social side, I still do not have a business. My business is finally tangible when I have a client, an invoice, a finished product, and a receivable. Once this physical side is complete, then you could say that I finally have a business. The tangible result of a finished product, a customer and a paid invoice, is the expression of the manifestation of the idea on the physical side and this side takes the longest time of all three sides to complete. This is the side where the "rubber hits the road" as it has the most distinctions and requires more time than the previous processes.

In this way, we work with our whole system, utilizing the mental, social, and physical sides. Although we start with the general structure and overview of AIR, we must also be awake to the entire process activated by FIRE causing reactions by WATER.

This process prepares the ideas of AIR to be received by EARTH. With only ideas, the world would not manifest new things. With only EARTH, the world would not change much. With only FIRE, we would not be able to sustain anything as everything would be consumed. With only WATER, everything would be washed away or muddied and confused.

When the mental awareness is maturely developed, it has the ability to be interdependent. While it can be objective, it is thoroughly in touch with the beauty of life and the pain and suffering of others. The mental AIR-preferred person sits above the rest of the elements, and in so doing has the advantage of seeing things without obstructions.

We need ideas, we need actions, we need reactions, and we need the building and manifestation of things tangible. The process of using the social elements of FIRE and WATER engages us in the actions and reactions of the elemental dynamics, and activates the feedback we need to build something new, something that is manifested in the EARTH element.

- To fulfill our destiny and lead a well-tempered life, we can think of AIR as energy that expands upward toward ether, or, as the expression goes, "as above, so below," we reach upward to draw downward. We start with an idea.
- FIRE, as one of the connectors to the idea, transforms WATER into gas expanding outward and upward toward AIR.

- WATER, as the second connector, moving outward and downward as it flows, shapes and transforms the idea of AIR with the solidness of EARTH, turning it into more of a fluid form so it can be shaped into something new.
- Then, EARTH, as a downward flow of energy, consolidates all the elements into a new form that addresses the current reality.

Adapted from my first book, *Natural to My Soul*[5], the process could look as follows:

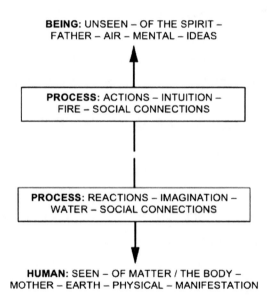

BEING: UNSEEN – OF THE SPIRIT – FATHER – AIR – MENTAL – IDEAS

PROCESS: ACTIONS – INTUITION – FIRE – SOCIAL CONNECTIONS

PROCESS: REACTIONS – IMAGINATION – WATER – SOCIAL CONNECTIONS

HUMAN: SEEN – OF MATTER / THE BODY – MOTHER – EARTH – PHYSICAL – MANIFESTATION

Using this structure to view the flow of life within ourselves, we appear to have a number of aspects working within us. We have the aspect of spirit, which we cannot see, and we have that part of us that is matter, which is of the EARTH and which is tangible and seen.

---

5   Gault, D. *Natural to My Soul*. Toronto: Wellness Training Services. 2011.

The EARTH part of us comes from "human," which is from the Latin root *humus*, meaning "of the earth," and is tangible and visible. The unseen "being" part of ourselves is of the spirit—our essences, our character, our moral compass.

We use the great elements (as they are referred to in the yoga world) of AIR, FIRE, WATER, and EARTH to bring our ideas out of the realm of concepts and abstraction and we strive to convert them into physical realities.

When coaching yourself to wellness, one of the most important considerations in evolving and in sorting out your life and your problems is to know what you are after (AIR).

When you know this, the actions you take and the reactions you feel will trigger a more comprehensive problem-solving process to assist you in moving from your current reality to your goal, dream, or outcome.

If you did not have a physical form (EARTH), you could not register and interpret your experiences (WATER) and form some basis for acting on them (FIRE). In registering your reactions (WATER) through your sensate body (EARTH), you decide what the experience means and how to relate to it, thereby linking the experience to the idea itself.

Are you solving your problem and moving toward your objective (AIR) or are you avoiding the problem and remaining in the same place? If you are engaged in solving your problem, you should notice that the tension within your body (EARTH), your emotions (WATER), and your thinking mind (AIR) disappears through your focused actions (FIRE).

If you avoid your problems, then the tension will remain. Sometimes the tension may be stronger and sometimes weaker, but it will be continuous as it looks for a resolution to the problem and a consequent release from the tension.

In registering and deciding about these experiences, your life starts to take shape. You and others should be able to see your outcome manifested in specific and measurable ways because a change has taken place in you or in some aspect of your life. When these patterns show up consistently over time, you will know that you have started to identify both your core psychological elements, which are strong in you, with your least preferred elements of expression that needed to be developed for you to grow into a more fully mature and well-rounded individual.

In my own case, as a mature student who was totally social and subjective, after the death of my first husband at the age of twenty-seven, I decided to develop my mental side and went to university. I wanted to marry an educated man and eventually married a physicist who understood academics and supported me in my efforts while we both raised our children in our blended marriage. I became less social and subjective as the elements were being more developed within. I am, however, still predominately a social-sided person, but I have now the advantage of more maturity of expression on the mental and physical sides of myself. This process of development is what Jung recommends for each of us so that we can become more "whole" individuals. We need to have all the elements activated, honed, and available to us, but we will always have a preferred one. In my case, it is the social side.

If, as AIR-preferred people, others experience us as too detached, floating above the world like a cloud in rarefied air unencumbered by physical limitations, we may come across as arrogant and too full of ourselves. If this is how we come across, Mother Nature, or some life lesson, will most likely show up for us, which could lead to opportunities for others to deflate, humiliate us, or bring us down. We do not tend to have much sympathy for downfalls that are brought on by arrogance. It is human nature to have feelings of resentment about others when they seem to feel that they can live above the law and take what is not theirs to take.

Moving into the FIRE of social relationships requires a commitment to the ongoing development of our capabilities. We also must believe in ourselves and have the spirituality and the drive to succeed. Learning to use the tools of the FIRE and WATER elements requires that we consistently interact in a conscious way by asking ourselves, "Am I moving toward my goal, dream, or outcome?" If we are not, then we need to reflect on what we have learned and plan how to move in our chosen direction. In this way we are making distinctions based on real-life experience and turning our feelings of failure into feedback.

When the four elements expressing the mental, social-mental, social-physical, and physical sides are dynamically and systematically in harmony, our total being expresses itself in a more congruent and mature way.

HOW TO RECOGNIZE "AIR" MOMENTS WHEN AIR IS NOT YOUR NATURAL PREFERENCE

When AIR is not your natural preference and it is underdeveloped or unfamiliar, it can be inappropriately expressed as overly detached or as overly compassionate. For example, emotions from a recently ended relationship may cause you to project anger and fear onto any potential new partner. Your disposition that normally is open and friendly now expresses itself as detached and aloof. An example of an inappropriate compassionate expression might be to give away money and personal things without consideration for your own needs. You fail to build yourself into the equation, putting everyone else's needs before your own.

You can recognize that an underdeveloped element is affecting you when people comment that your actions are out of character and "not like you." This would be the most evident way for you to know that you are having a "moment" in the development of an element that is not natural or fully developed.

COACHING TOOLS TO ENLIVEN MENTAL AWARENESS

When looking at issues in our lives, we have to start to flush out areas to focus on and to start to work with. We can do this by asking ourselves some questions. The table below is an example of how to go about the start of this process.

QUESTION	RESPONSE	NEXT STEPS
What goal are you working on right now?	Getting a new job.	Explore processes involved in finding a new job.
Where are you in relation to reaching the goal?	I've only just started exploring my options.	Explore options. Get support.
What keeps you from reaching the goal?	Too much to do.	Break down processes into small manageable steps to keep focused.
How will you know you are getting closer to or have reached the goal?	When I have interviews set up.	Explore processes involved in setting up interviews. Establish targets and timetables.

Now, answer the questions for yourself:

- What goal am I working on right now?
- Where am I in relation to reaching the goal?

- What keeps me from reaching the goal?
- How will I know I am getting closer to or have reached the goal?

Continue using your mental awareness to become more focused. You might want to look at other areas of your life as you begin the journey to coaching yourself to wellness. For example, using what I call the "holistic framework," identify how you would rate yourself on a scale of 1 (poor) to 10 (strong) in each of the states in the inventory below.

INVENTORY OF STATES SELF-ASSESSMENT

Mental state – Do I feel alert, have good concentration, and make appropriate decisions? Am I curious and open-minded? Am I satisfied with my interest in personal growth? Am I being challenged?

| 1 | 2 | 3 | 4 | 5 | 6 | 7 | 8 | 9 | 10 |

Social state – Are my relationships with others healthy, constructive, trusting, and supportive? Do I feel I can express my feelings? Do I accept other's feelings? Do I feel I have self-confidence, self-knowledge, and self-control? Am I able to feel empathy, intimacy, and sensitivity with others?

| 1 | 2 | 3 | 4 | 5 | 6 | 7 | 8 | 9 | 10 |

Physical state – Do I have a healthy weight, flexible joints, energy, stamina, strength, and vitality? Do I consume a proper diet with little or no daily intake of caffeine, alcohol, and sweets? Do I manage my finances well, cope well with change, and have an orderly home environment? Am I satisfied with my job/career?

| 1 | 2 | 3 | 4 | 5 | 6 | 7 | 8 | 9 | 10 |

Spiritual state – Do I feel I have a purpose in my life? Do I have inner peace, hope, courage, and joy? Do I have a positive outlook and a commitment to higher principles? Am I nourished by nature? Do I spend time in meditation and on reflection? Do I feel grateful and involve myself in creative activities?

| 1 | 2 | 3 | 4 | 5 | 6 | 7 | 8 | 9 | 10 |

Which state speaks the loudest to you and would you like to be the start of your coaching journey: mental, social, physical, or spiritual?

Keep focused. Next, addressing the state that most speaks out to you right now, ask yourself and answer the question: "What would it do for me if I were to improve the rating?"

I AS CENTER OF MY UNIVERSE	STATE OF FOCUS	SMART GOAL	SUPPORT/ RESOURCES
NOW?			
FIVE YEARS FROM NOW?			
IN 100 YEARS, I WANT TO BE REMEMBERED FOR WHAT?			

Continue your thinking and consider the following as you work toward creating for yourself a SMART goal: S – specific, M – measurable, A – achievable, R – relevant, and T – timed.

Change is not easy. Changing our beliefs about our self or changing a habit or pattern we are used to is a great challenge for everyone. There are many things that can get in the way of change, but one thing is for sure: Our first block is what we know and do now and knew and did in the past. We cannot change anything until we are ready to give up the old ways we have done things in the past. When we move toward our goal, we will encounter obstacles along the way that will try to sabotage us in an effort to keep us in the same place.

For mental-sided people, one of their obstacles can be that they feel they no longer need to act after thinking. The thinking is enough. They do not feel that they need the support of others because they are independent and above most people's standards as they go about their work with no time for other people's priorities. They have not yet learned that you have to do it yourself and you cannot do it alone. They are fearful that they may lose their identity or change the way they think about themselves. They are uncomfortable about being vulnerable and certainly are not well-developed in expression of feelings.

Techniques and suggestions for AIR people would be to get more in touch with their bodies. One great series of poses to do is some rounds of the Sun Salutation. Here, they reach up and then draw down. Another technique for the AIR-preferred mental-sided is to massage their ears, stimulating their body systems through their ear reflexes.

The next few pages provide some tools and techniques for mental-sided AIR people.

YOGA POSTURES AND BREATHING EXERCISES TO ENLIVEN AIR EXPRESSION

These yoga poses will assist the AIR element in its development of compassion, tolerance, and humility, the metaphysical aspects of Anahata, the fourth center of awareness in the heart area. To develop metaphysical awareness in this area, the following flow is useful.

1. Stand straight and tall with your hands in prayer position at the heart chakra. Visualize the heart and see your loving energy expanding out into the world, filling the world with loving energy and intentions as you inhale and reach upward.

2. Notice your breathing and sense the whole universe within you. Feel that connection as you reach your hands upward and bend your body backward slightly.

3. Tap into those finer energies and breathe them back down to Mother Earth as you exhale and gently go into a forward bend, bending your knees slightly.

4. Feel the energy coming up from Mother Earth into your body, into your heart, and into your mind as you return to a standing position. Inhale and again reach your arms upward, bending your body backward slightly.

5. Exhale and return to the prayer position. Close your eyes and feel the effects of this movement. Experience it. Feel this energy vibrating within and around you. You are the connection. You are the vital link in the evolution of world consciousness, drawing from above to below and from below to above.

Perform this flow three to six times.

EAR REFLEXOLOGY TO CALM AND BALANCE AIR EXPRESSION

Reflexology of the ears will help you to calm the mind and develop appropriate use of your attention to regain a sense of purpose and direction.

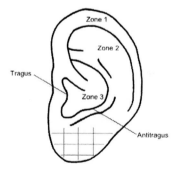

1. **Warm-up.** Start by rubbing your hands together, generating heat in the palms. Cup the ears with your warmed hands. Next:

- Hold the tops of the ears (zone 1) between the thumbs and fingers. Stretch upward three times.
- Slide halfway down the edge of the ears to the midpoint between the tops and the lobes, then stretch outward three times.
- Slide down to the lobes and stretch downward three times.

2. **Zone 1** – Relax tension in reflexes related to excretion and respiratory systems. With your index fingers behind and your thumbs in front, press and release slowly along zone 1 from the tops of the ears toward the lobes. Stop as you get near the lobes and work your way back. Repeat this three times. (Alternatively you may work with your index fingers in front and your thumbs behind.)

3. **Zone 2** – Relax tension in reflexes related to skeletal system. Continue your pressure point massage, covering zone 2 thoroughly. Repeat three times.

4. **Zone 3** – Relax tension in reflexes related to internal organs. Work bowl-shaped zone 3 thoroughly the same way to stimulate reflexes to internal organs and body parts such as the stomach, liver, colon, lungs, and heart.

5. **Lobe** – Relax tension in reflexes related to head area. Work the lobes with the same two fingers, pressing and massaging the entire area. Imagine each lobe as divided into nine sections (three lines down and three lines across) and work each one thoroughly. This stimulates reflexes to the head, eyes, teeth, jaws, ears, and tonsil area.

6. **Tragus and antitragus** – Relax tension in reflexes related to inflammations and fevers. Applying the same pressure point massage technique, work the two protrusions on the ear called the tragus and the antitragus.

- Support your head in your palms, your index fingers vertically behind the ears and your other fingers vertically in front of the ears. Massage this area by rubbing up and down; this stimulates and relaxes the jaw muscles and bones in this area.

- Next, place your index fingers into the ear cavities as if you were trying to block out sounds. Quickly jiggle the index fingers vigorously up and down; this stimulates the ear channels.

7. **Conclusion.** End by bending the ears inward toward the head as if they were flaps to be closed. Once again cup your ears, then close your eyes and take a couple of deep breaths, inhaling through your nose and exhaling slowly through your mouth. Pause to feel the effects of this circulatory work on your body. Notice the calming effect throughout your whole system.

THE MATURE AIR ELEMENT BRINGS CREATIVE AND FOCUSED ATTENTION

Creative and focused attention comes to people who use their mental powers wisely. This gift of attention allows the mental awareness its capacity for cutting through the illusion of false attachments and lets us see the truths that can set us free.

When the AIR expression is balanced and maturely developed, we express intelligence, compassion, forgiveness, and humility while living a life of humanitarian service.

We start our clarification and coaching process with the mental function of AIR: *"Who am I?"*

Next, we activate the process with actions of the social-mental function of FIRE: *"What should I do?"*

CHAPTER **5**

THE FIRE ELEMENT

When we work with the energies of the third chakra, Manipura, we are dealing with the development of our inner strengths, our will, and our personal power. The FIRE element is action-oriented. Following is an example of a self-expression by a FIRE-preferred person we will call "Janet" in response to a question during her coaching to gain greater self-awareness.

The question was the same one asked of Richard in Chapter 4: *"How would you describe yourself, your strengths, and your gifts, and how you strive to share these with the world?"*

WHAT IS A FIRE TYPE LIKE?

The FIRE element relates to social-mental awareness and links ideas to actions. Janet is a person whose preference is the FIRE element. She seeks to solve problems and move ideas forward by finding solutions. In her words:

"*I see things quickly. Answers come to me just as if I am breathing them in. I don't know where they come from, they just come and I act on them. I am faced with a problem and then I can see an answer. I move on that information and take steps that cause things to happen. For me, it is not just the idea that is important as much as the actions to move the idea forward.*

"*Often I have been in a room full of people and have never understood why they just sit there and do and say nothing. Are they not interested? Don't they care? I always seem to be the one who kicks into gear first. My motors are revving. 'Let's get going,' I would think to myself. 'Why all this sitting around chatting or arguing about what to do? Here's an idea, let's just do it.'*

"*Why I always have to be the one to cause things to happen, I don't know, but that is how I've always been. It's as if people like me don't have enough time in our life, and we have to focus and stay active so we don't waste any of it. My energy appears high to others because I simply take what's in front of me and act on it. I can see immediate things that can be done and how they can come together to achieve goals. I have no problem in finding immediate answers to questions that others scratch their heads over. I don't get bogged down with past data, future daydreaming, or emotional issues, so it's easy for me to be immediate and focused.*

"*Sometimes people take offense because they think I'm overbearing or arrogant, but that is not what I'm trying to be. I simply want to get moving on things so there is no time wasted. If I am really focused, I can appear to be impatient and can get frustrated when things don't go fast enough for me. If meetings get too boring for me and my approaches aren't appreciated, I tend to shut down and want to get out of there in a hurry.*

"*I've always been very handy and can work mechanical things easily, fix things quickly, work with tools putting things together, whatever. If there is something in front of me requiring fixing, organizing or moving, I can do it. I don't see what gives other people problems around things like that. 'Just do it!' is an expression that suits me very well.*

"One thing I have noticed about myself in the course of my life is that I sometimes don't hold onto things. I have made and lost lots of money, possessions, and relationships in the past. Things tend to disappear around me from time to time. I also notice that I may not take as good care of my body as some of my colleagues do of theirs.

"Oh, I know that I may take on too many projects, but when people ask me for my advice, I find it hard to pull away, taking such pleasure in problem-solving as I do. Because of this nature, I may become overloaded from time to time and not even notice that I've done it again. Once in awhile, my body may break down as if to say, that's enough! I would like it if I could register this awareness a little earlier in the game so that I don't have to be ill in order to take a rest. I'm working on this.

"I'm also working on having more patience with other people's paces. I know that other people don't see moving on things as vitally important as I do, and so I am trying to understand their process and to work more closely in alignment with them. But you have to know that I'm like a horse at the starting gate, champing at the bit. It is as hard for me to slow myself down as it might be for others to pick up speed to keep up with me.

"My mission on this planet is to serve others by providing them with my ability to see clearly what needs to be done next and to come up with creative approaches for solving problems. As long as I'm contributing to projects and people in this way, I feel that I am using my talents and skills wisely. If there is a problem to be solved, call me."

HOW TO RECOGNIZE AND DEAL WITH PITFALLS OF THE FIRE TYPE

Vigilance is the gift of the FIRE person. In its mature form, this element uses its focused energy to bring benefits to humanity rather than to serve the self. When FIRE operates from instinctive forces without rational thought, it can create a superficial world that soon tumbles from its lack of preparation or foundation. This is the pitfall of the FIRE element without development and benefit of the other three elements.

Feeling that they have no time to waste, fast-paced FIRE people use their energy to produce a continuous flow of output. Moving from one busy activity to another, FIRE-preferred people get impatient when things are not moving fast enough in their lives. They get bored with uninteresting details, too many numbers, or the limitations of parameters. They would rather just keep moving onto the next set of actions.

They have to be careful that they do not build a house without a foundation, as the physical side is not being tended to and may not continue to support them. Neglecting their physical world, FIRE people consume everything in their mad pursuits. Jung says man is not a machine in the sense that he cannot constantly maintain the same output of work. He can only meet the demands of outer necessity in an ideal way if he is also adapted to his own inner world, that is to say, if he is in harmony with himself.[6]

When we are not in harmony with our total system, those areas of growth that we need for balance are often the areas we find most boring and want to gloss over. Feeling important because we are so busy, we lose sight of quality-of-life issues, and eventually the body, the relationships, and the physical world we live in break down. Driven by an unconscious force, the energy of the FIRE-dominant intensifies and sharpens its focus on the goal. In the book *Philosophy of the Unconscious,* Eduard von Hartmann states the will has an unconscious inner purpose that drives all the life forces in the direction of its aim. These drives, if not stopped

---

6   Jung, C.G. *Contributions to Analytical Psychology.* New York: Harcourt Brace & Co. 1928.

and analyzed, will continue to exert pressure in the human personality beyond the controls of the rational conscious mind.[7]

If the qualities of the FIRE element remain imbalanced and immature, a life of conflict and loss is often evidenced. The instinctive drive causes irrational decisions and constant changes that result in headstrong and impulsive actions. The job never seems to get done. Relationships suffer because frustrations and differences of opinions quickly turn into quarrels.

Two mental waves can capture the immature FIRE expression. The first wave is expressed as arrogance as the mind believes it can do anything. When success is obtained, the overzealous FIRE becomes conceited and hypocritical. Full of its own importance, it continues to be driven by its own force without regard for others. The FIRE-dominant leaves others feeling used and abused.

The second wave is expressed as ignorance. Acting childishly, the imbalanced FIRE expression learns nothing from its experiences. With little judgment or understanding of right and wrong, FIRE grasps onto everything, and holds little regard for the environment or for others. It exchanges short-term comfort for long-term pain and frequently finds itself returning to the circumstance it thought it could escape, repeating a similar pattern. When the aims of the unchecked FIRE take hold of our actions, tension is created in the body and mind due to moving too rapidly toward fixed points.

When we operate from a balanced expression of the FIRE element, we can rely on our actions to bring direct results. The FIRE element, to express its spiritual aspects, strives to open to a more conscious, rational, and sensitive approach for service to humankind. There are times when the force of the FIRE element is necessary to stir things up. However,

---

7   Von Hartmann, Eduard. *Philosophy of the Unconscious: Speculative Results According to the Inductive Method of Physical Science.* London: Routledge & Kegan Paul Ltd. 1950.

there are also times when people require a "softer" approach. It is the struggle of the FIRE element as it matures to see, feel, and understand the approach that is best for others involved.

HOW TO RECOGNIZE "FIRE" MOMENTS WHEN FIRE IS NOT YOUR NATURAL PREFERENCE

When FIRE is not your natural preference and it is undeveloped or unfamiliar, it can be inappropriately expressed as destructive anger or intense and gripping impatience.

For example, the grief of losing a loved one and the stress of facing the world alone may result in displays of angry outbursts at times when your behavior normally would have been different. An example of intense and gripping impatience is when you find that the activities of your life and the demands of others have pushed you outside your comfort zone. Suddenly caught in slow traffic, you are beside yourself with impatience that is felt intensely throughout your body, and nothing you do relieves the tension or alters your focus.

You can recognize that an underdeveloped element is affecting you when people see you in ways that differ from how they normally perceive you. This would be a "moment" of development in an element that is not your preference.

COACHING TOOLS TO ENLIVEN SOCIAL-MENTAL AWARENESS

When striving to change our habits and patterns, we need to identify and set goals that are determined by and supportive of our life's mission and purpose. It is not just about getting things done; more importantly, it is about using a systematic approach to understand the natural parameters around us and to make step-by-step plans with assigned criteria and timelines for monitoring results to reach our goals. This will help FIRE to resist its "shoot-from-the-hip" approach, its first and automatic response for doing things.

To tap into a more spiritual expression of who you are, ask yourself: *"Does this goal support my life's purpose and direction? What are the consequences of my actions on others?"*

As you move from the idea of a goal to the process of achieving the goal, you can maintain your focus and feel in control of your process by defining anything that may be getting in your way. Ask yourself the following questions:

- What is happening now?"
- How often does this happen?
- When does this tend to happen?
- What are the effects?

The greater the degree to which you understand your process and analyze your journey along the way, the greater the degree to which you can take ownership of and responsibility for solving problems— closing the gap between your current reality and your future goal or dream.

When applying the holistic framework to identify my own goal at the beginning of the year, I was surprised to find that my spiritual side had the lowest score. (This was especially surprising as I was attending a meditation retreat when I rated myself on my mental, social, physical, and spiritual sides.) Once I became aware that something was lacking in my life—a clear purpose for my age and stage in life—I continued to flush out the problem by asking myself questions. These questions led me to greater clarity and my problem statement became: I like to travel and I am not traveling.

So, it then became more obvious to me that I needed to focus my goal on a desired future state to increase my level of spiritual satisfaction—close the gap between the current reality of thinking of myself as a traveler and that I am not traveling. Now, the future outcome of being a traveler can pull me toward my vision, or goal, and energize me, thus boosting my spiritual rating.

Continuing to flush out my future state, I also realized that I not only needed to be a traveler, but that I needed to share my wisdom, knowledge, and skills with others. Because of my age, I knew I needed to take a bigger step and not waste any more time in getting my information out into the world. What was I waiting for anyway?

To keep yourself focused and help you to do more analysis, you can use DADS:

- **D** – Define the present state and the desired state.
- **A** – Analyze the problem (the gap between the two states).
- **D** – Determine where and/or how the problem originated.
- **S** – State and restate the problem so you become very clear about what it is you want to coach yourself to move toward.

In this way, we build in a rational approach by analyzing ourselves and circumstances rather than letting our instincts run our activities in life. This is intelligent intuition, where intuition provides answers, but before actions are incorporated, benefits and consequences are reviewed.

For FIRE people, one obstacle on the social-mental side can be that they scatter their efforts, often change directions, and act as if there is only today. By operating in this fashion, they can easily get bowled over by the moment. Another obstacle can be that as they push outward to accomplish things, they often forget about the necessary counterbalance activities of rest and repair. In nature, there is both an inward flow and an outward flow. We cannot keep flowing outward without an inward flow and not expect some imbalance to show up in us.

YOGA POSTURES AND BREATHING EXERCISES TO ENLIVEN FIRE EXPRESSION

These Yoga poses will assist the FIRE element in its development of vigilance, the proper use of intuition, and the intelligent and rational use of a strong, forceful will. These are the metaphysical higher aspects of the solar plexus, or Manipura chakra, the third center of awareness.

Warrior pose. The Warrior pose assists in the coordination of the body with the mind by use of focused tension throughout the posture flow.

1. Stand with your arms out at shoulder height. Spread your feet apart and bend your right knee, ensuring it does not extend beyond your toes. Looking at your right hand, hold the pose for thirty seconds or so as you concentrate on the mighty energy of the warrior. Feel the tension in your legs, arms, and shoulders as you focus on truth, being, and light. Be vigilant, concentrate, focus, and breathe.

2. Now bring your left hand over to meet your right hand. Interlace your fingers and point the index fingers outward, then lift your hands upward as if to shoot an arrow vertically into the sky. Look up. Hold the position for a few seconds. Breathe.

3. Repeat the pose, this time bending the left knee and looking up toward the left hand.

Resting pose. Follow the warrior pose with the resting pose, also known as the corpse pose.

1. Lie on your back with your feet flopped outward and your arms and palms slightly away from your body with the palms turned upward. Feel the points of contact of your body with the floor. Become aware of your body in its resting state. Surrender into the floor, letting your body melt into a silent state of deep relaxation.

2. If you feel any tension in your body, focus your breath on that area and breathe into it as you imagine sending loving energy to the tension, letting it melt away.

When FIRE learns to follow each warrior action with a deep rest, it learns to balance its energy flow, to maintain inner harmony, and to use its energy in powerful ways for service to the world.

HAND REFLEXOLOGY TO COOL AND BALANCE FIRE EXPRESSION

Reflexology of the hands helps to cool the emotions and develop greater vigilance. Follow the steps below to increase circulation and relax tensions in the reflexes related to the body.

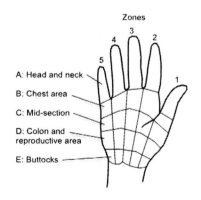

1. Warm-up. Start by rubbing and wringing your hands to generate warmth—as if trying to squeeze out something.

2. A – Relax tension in reflexes related to head and neck area. Place your right hand palm-upward in your left hand, supporting the fingers with your left fingers behind and your left thumb on top. Starting at the baby finger, press your left thumb into the pad, giving it a pressure point massage at the fingertip. Then, slowly thumb-walk (apply your thumb in a press-release manner) along the length of the finger until you reach the base. Work the finger along three lines: once along each side and once along the middle. Do this procedure three times on each finger and the thumb.

3. Webs – Relax tension in reflexes related to neck and shoulder area. Grab, in turn, each web—the flesh between your fingers and between your index finger and thumb—and thoroughly massage the area, ending with a slight tug.

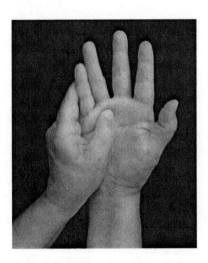

4. B – Relax tension in reflexes related to chest, breast, and lung areas. Hold your right hand so the palm faces you and grasp it with your left thumb on the palm side and your left fingers behind. Starting where sections B and C meet, thumb-walk upward in the valleys between the (metacarpal) bones. Work all four valleys three times.

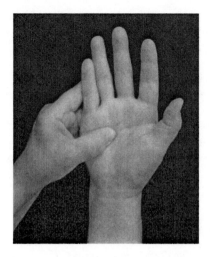

5. C – Relax tension in reflexes related to stomach, pancreas, liver, and spleen areas. Thumb-walk section C, working the entire area thoroughly three times.

6. D – Relax tension in reflexes related to colon and reproductive system. Thumb-walk section D, working the entire area thoroughly three times.

7. E – Relax tension in reflexes related to buttocks area. Locate the fleshy butt-shaped area at the base of your palm just above the wrist and below section D. Grasping your hand with your left four fingers, use your left thumb to thumb-walk this area thoroughly. Repeat three times.

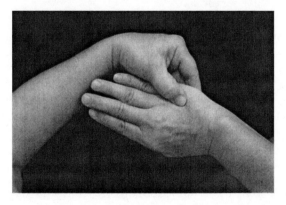

8. Top of hand – Relax tension in reflexes related to upper back. Turn your right hand palm-downward and thumb-walk along the valleys between the bones on the top of the hand. Work from the base of each finger to the wrist area. Repeat three times.

9. Wrist – Relax tension in reflexes related to groin-lymphatic area. Thumb-walk along the wrist area from the wrist bone on one side to the wrist bone on the other side. Repeat three times.

10. Lateral side of hand – Relax tension in reflexes related to peripheral areas such as outer arms, hips, and legs. Grab the flesh on the outer edge of the hand at the base of the baby finger, your thumb on the palm side and your fingers on the top side. (Alternatively you may place your thumb on the top side and your fingers on the palm side.) Use a pinch-and-release motion to work toward the wrist, covering zone 5 thoroughly.

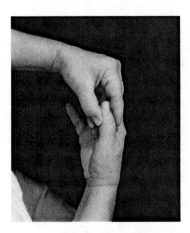

11. Medial side of hand – Relax tension in reflexes related to spine area. Grasp the right thumb between the thumb and the index finger of your left hand, the thumb on the outside. Thumb-walk along the area from the nail to the wrist. Slide the thumb back up to the nail and repeat a few times.

12. Conclusion. Shake your hands vigorously, then wring and rub them together as you did when you started. Repeat the entire procedure on your left hand. After completing both hands, massage them with lotion while taking a couple of deep breaths, inhaling through your nose and exhaling slowly through your mouth. Pause, close your eyes, and feel the effects of this circulatory work throughout your whole system. Feel the gentle cooling and calming effects on your emotional state.

THE MATURE FIRE ELEMENT BRINGS VIGILANCE

When FIRE is maturely developed, its dynamic and fiery energy of intuition descends like autumn leaves from a tree, dropping sparks of inspiration. The gift of the FIRE element is the vigilant ever-ready actions of the warrior in enlisting the aid of others to bring ideas forward out of the realm of concepts.

When appropriate expression of FIRE's will is used to dispense original approaches to problems, insights come as easily as breathing air. Leading others is conveyed through expressive vitality. Trusting the flow of intuition is used in a conscious approach for illuminating the world and achieving spiritual success.

Step 1. AIR: *"Who am I?"*

Step 2. FIRE: *"What should I do?"*

Step 3. WATER: *"Who and/or what else is involved and how am I feeling about all this?"*

"If I change the way I do things, how will it affect others? How will I deal with a change that alters the way I've done things in the past?"

We have to be prepared to change the system that we have lived in the past, and this requires both effort and foresight to prepare us to deal with how we may undermine or sabotage ourselves along the way.

CHAPTER **6**

THE WATER ELEMENT

When we work with the energies of the second chakra, Svadisthana, we are dealing with the development of our reflective natures. Our reflective natures are described best by the WATER element. Following is an example of a self-expression by a WATER-preferred person we will call "Danielle"—me—in response to a question during self-coaching to gain greater self-awareness.

The question was the same one asked of Richard (AIR, Chapter 4) and Janet (FIRE, Chapter 5): *"How would I describe myself, my strengths, and my gifts, and how I strive to share these with the world?"*

WHAT IS A WATER TYPE LIKE?

The WATER element is the part of us that deals with our reactions to the ideas of AIR and the actions of FIRE. These reactions stimulate a catalytic response for expansion and growth, and link the mind to the physical element of EARTH. Through our reactions, we reflect on our emotions and our imagination is stimulated. In the second chakra, we learn how to develop our imagination and how to express our feelings appropriately. Our desire to affiliate and cooperate with others leads us to pursue intimate and mature relationships.

The WATER element relates to social-physical awareness that links ideas and actions to our reactions. I am a person whose preference is the WATER element.

"As a child, I was naturally drawn to mediate problems in the family as I was able to understand all sides of an issue. I wanted to ensure that everyone felt heard and that they worked toward some mutually-satisfying resolution. Never taking a clear stand on anything—except that people should get along with each other—I lacked a strong identity of my own and seemed to go pleasantly along with the flow of things. People probably didn't know me very well because I would show one aspect of myself to this person and another aspect to that person. After reading a novel, I would take on the characteristics of the heroine.

"I spoke up for the causes of others, often putting their needs above my own. I didn't feel that my needs were that important because they would keep changing. As I matured and started learning from my actions and behaviors, I eventually registered feedback from that side of my personality that relates more to the EARTH element. I began to see that by taking this type of action, I would be more certain to get feedback from others that would nurture me and make me happy. If I took a different set of actions, I would be more likely to be jarred by the reactions I would get from others and this would make me unhappy.

"Being WATER-dominant, it was not unusual for me to pick up the feelings of those around me. Sometimes I wasn't sure if the feelings I had were my own or if they belonged to someone else. I was like a sponge and absorbed feelings into me—WATER and EARTH can make for murky

water. *Having a strong sense of social justice and being especially sensitive to the underdog, I was quick to pick up the slightest word, gesture, or feeling that could hurt someone. I then had to make things better for that person.*

"*After the death of my first husband, my FIRE element kicked in full-force, and for the first time in my life I started to demand things for myself. Because I was new to FIRE in my late twenties, FIRE was expressed in an immature fashion. I rudely offended people who I loved in ways that I would never do today without serious regrets. Once I got used to FIRE burning in me, I had to learn to temper it so it wouldn't come up in unexpected ways and throw me off-guard. I needed to be able to draw on its use, but I also wanted to have choices around using the force of my own will. Being sensitive to others, I knew I would have to pay a price in terms of guilt for unconscious use of this force since FIRE is not my preferred element.*

"*My least developed element is AIR, which could provide me with the objectivity I need to stop personalizing the world around me. Over the years, I have learned to go up to the mountaintop in the form of meditation to develop my AIR element. Although I love the mountaintop and meditation, I also know deep inside that I cannot stay there very long as my calling is to connect with people and their feelings. Here is where I belong, and this is how I can best use my gifts and talents. However, I now know from experience that I must go to the mountaintop from time to time to release from my sponge all the emotions it has absorbed as well as to remind myself that things looks better from a broader perspective. But my place and role on Earth is connecting with others in ways that help to bring about empowerment. This I have learned only through diligent work on myself and with accepting and including myself in the formula of caring for people in the world. I strive hard not to take on the ways of others, but to learn how I can be true to myself.*

"Because I have a strong affinity to EARTH, whatever I do must have practical applications. I like to mix the world of EARTH (the body) and all its humanness with the flow of WATER (feelings), the force of FIRE (actions), and the objectivity of AIR (ideas) for developing all aspects of my human potential. In doing this, I am naturally fulfilling my life's mission. This is how I would describe my work: fulfilling my spiritual mission on the planet."

HOW TO RECOGNIZE AND DEAL WITH PITFALLS OF THE WATER TYPE

Our spiritual purpose is to incarnate higher spiritual expressions into the body of matter by use of the four elements found in the individual personality. By tapping into and developing these elements, the spiritual side requires that the individual develop conscious "knowing of self." The WATER element brings this process to a more personal experience through interpreting and reflecting on our feelings. The WATER element acts as a catalyst for the other elements, ensuring that the proper use of expressions of each element is sensitive to the entirety of expressions of all four elements.

Without a well-developed and mature WATER element, the other elements are not as realized as they could be. The registration of our feelings is a vital and catalytic basis of information. Assisting in the spiritual growth and development process, WATER mediates the tensions triggered by the ideas of AIR and the actions of FIRE, and prepares the way for the integration of both AIR and FIRE with the EARTH element. When, for example, we have feelings of anger arising from our FIRE element, we can act constructively by letting people know what is happening with us. We do not attack, but instead we share the basis for these feelings with them. In this way, we are providing feedback as a participant in life, and perhaps assisting others to see that they may be overstepping some boundaries.

When we are depressed, our sensate bodies are telling us to express ourselves, to stand up for ourselves, to bring out in us the warrior represented by our FIRE element that we are failing to use because our WATER element is damping our will.

When we are confused about "who" we are, or when we have too grand a picture of our own importance, our sensate body feels stressed as the mind strives to clarify what is happening. The mind would not bother to try to clarify if the feelings of confusion were not present.

Reactions triggered by the feelings help to surface differences for mediation of tensions between the ideas and the actions. This mediation assists in the manifestation of results by being an interface for processing data and preparing the way for the physical distinctions of EARTH.

In many ways, the WATER element acts as our social conscience in life, assisting us in dealing with issues that affect us. Everything tangible comes through awareness of sensations of feelings in the body. Our body is nature's gift to us. This is our feedback machine. We cannot change unless we get, give, and work with this important part of ourselves. With feedback from both the internal and the external worlds comes increased awareness of the whole system. With increased awareness, we become more conscious.

"Knowing ourselves" is developed through life experiences and analysis. If we do not learn things on our own and open up to what life presents us, we will repeatedly face challenges and be presented with opportunities to grow. Our lessons will come to us in one way or another, but until we comprehend the lessons, we will continue to be presented with opportunities for growth. That is nature's way of forcing us into awakening and expanding our consciousness. Tension awakens us out of the relative world where we are not awake. With tension, we become "at-attention" or "at-tension." Out of the struggle between pain and pleasure, tension enlivens within us a need to broaden our awareness in order to awaken to greater consciousness and better choices.

- Tension = Pressure
- Pressure = Need for change
- Change = Adaptation
- Adaptation = Integration
- Integration = Broadening of consciousness
- Broadening of consciousness = Enlightened use of energies/ elements

The goal of yoga is Brahman Bhavanam—
to identify with Supreme Intelligence.

Our physical drives and impulses are channeled toward fulfillment of the soul. The soul is that invisible inner essence, inner memory, and inner desire that strives to push forward to serve humanity.

When we do not accept ourselves, we often fail to share our natural gifts with others. Self-acceptance comes from our awareness and appreciation of these gifts. As we develop more of our spiritual side, our natural gifts will shine through. When we maturely express the finer qualities of our four lower chakras, we naturally and easily enliven, integrate, and holistically expand ourselves and how we connect to the whole human family.

We pursue our holistic approach by focusing our attention on the needs of the community as a whole rather than on only our individual desires. To gently encourage the individual ego into higher self-expressions, we do not "instruct" the ego on what to do as this will only cause the ego to "dig in its heels" even more deeply and find reasons not to cooperate.

The ego is in a good position to resist change because of how it sets up things for us. Rather than rely on the ego, we need to invite all aspects of ourselves to participate by asking open-ended questions such as: *"What is the best solution for everyone in this situation, and how can I best assist with what I know and do well?"* In this way, the ego of the human self can comfortably begin to serve the higher spiritual self by using its own gifts and talents for service to humanity. Using its talents is something the ego would naturally like to do! Through reflection on the people and the activities that affect our lives and how our world is treating us, we trigger within us a process of more consciously deciding how we want to be when dealing with others.

When WATER-element people feel unsafe in their world, they hold themselves back. By stifling their natural tendencies, they fail to appreciate how creative and imaginative they can be. When fear prevents them from expressing themselves, they lack enthusiasm and withdraw from others.

Sometimes life presents us with a major crisis. Either this crisis provides an opportunity for personal growth and a calling to fulfill something through risk-taking, or the crisis intensifies our fears and sends us further inward until a fall occurs and we are forced into personal growth. One way or the other, we have to listen to Mother Nature.

HOW TO RECOGNIZE "WATER" MOMENTS WHEN WATER IS NOT YOUR NATURAL PREFERENCE

When WATER is not your natural preference and it is undeveloped and unfamiliar, it can take on various expressions. One of these expressions is to act very childlike. For example, you talk openly about an emotional event in your personal life when you usually do not discuss this type of thing with others. Or, suddenly you giggle and you put your hand to your mouth to stifle it, but the giggling continues and you are embarrassed. Another expression takes the form of inappropriate emotions. For example, you have been living in a foreign country for three months, and in preparation for returning home, you decide to close your bank account. Knowing you will not see the teller again, you say goodbye repeatedly three or four times—projecting your own personal sense of sadness and loss about your upcoming departure onto another person.

As in both types of examples, you display behavior that is not normal for you and people may comment that you are not "behaving like yourself."

COACHING TOOLS TO ENLIVEN SOCIAL-PHYSICAL AWARENESS

Using a planned structure to keep on track is critical to WATER-preferred people. One of their biggest challenges is to overcome their inability to say "no" as they fail to see that their own time and personal needs are as equally important as those of everyone else. They forget to put themselves into the equation.

Maintaining focus and keeping on track is a matter of identifying what is urgent and what is important at the start of each day. Time management and assertiveness skills are critical for WATER-preferred people when they coach themselves forward to achieve dreams, goals, and outcomes.

WATER-element people feel guilty if they do not give their time to others. They tend to neglect their own needs and priorities. Because of this, they require the tools of the physical side so they can identify and define their limitations, their parameters, and their available time.

Using time as a tool to your advantage, ask yourself: *"What can I do today to move toward my goal? What can I plan to do tomorrow? What about two weeks from today? What about a month from now?"* Putting a structure on their time is the best advice on processes for WATER-element people.

And learn to say "no." You can say it in constructive ways, such as: *"I'd love to help you with that, but I have to get this project done by the end of next week."* Or, something like, *"I can help you with that but not until later today."* In this way, you can still honor yourself at the same time that you feel good about helping someone else—when it is convenient for you and not at your expense.

FACTOR-OF-SUCCESS METHOD. This is one time-management tool that I have found to be helpful. At the start of each day, identify your priorities and list those things that are going to move you ahead and will bring you the greatest feeling of success. Assign each activity or task a rating of from 1 (highest) to 3 (lowest) on a scale of Urgency and on a scale of Importance. Then, multiply together the two ratings to find your priority with the greatest likelihood or factor of Success:

- Success = Urgency x Importance

For example, let's say that I have identified and rated three priorities for today:

- Association surveys: 2 for Urgency and 3 for Importance. Success = 2 x 3 = **6**
- Coaching program timeline: 1 for Urgency and 1 for Importance. Success = 1 x 1 = **1**
- Book project editing: 2 for Urgency and 1 for Importance. Success = 2 x 1 = **2**

In the example, the best thing for me to focus on first is the coaching program timeline as it rates 1 x 1 = 1. The next thing for me to do is to work on the book project editing as it rates 2 x 1 = 2. Last to work on is the association surveys as it rates 2 x 3 = 6.

Using this method, I can now see clearly what will bring me the greatest feeling of success, and that is where I should focus my attention and efforts. This will help me to stay on-track and keep me from going off on tangents. I have coached myself to success!

CATEGORIES-FOR-THE-WEEK METHOD. This is another method I use and find very helpful. At the start of each week, I list on flipchart paper everything coming in the week ahead that I can think of and should focus on. I make a list of categories, then list the items for each category. I have found that this is the easiest time-management tool I have ever learned to use that brings me the greatest satisfaction. Just listing items like this keeps me clearly focused. At the end of the week, I am always amazed at how much of my list was completed. In fact, I can honestly say that at least ninety percent of all of my lists have been completed at the end of each week in my thirty years of using this method—which I learned at my first corporate job from a very intense boss. I have tried many other time-management tools over the years, but this one remains my favorite and most satisfying.

Here is an example of what has resulted from the following open-statement that I use weekly to guide myself and set priorities:

Looking ahead at the coming week, I will feel good if at the end of the week I have accomplished:

Category 1 – Appointments	Category 2 – Telephone calls
1. Doctor	1. Book Master Mind
2. Hair dresser	2. Cancel eye examination
3. Exercise x 3	3. Group meeting call
4. Lunch for Sam	4. Coaching students
5. Cooking class	5. Call Gloria back

Category 3 – Workshops	Category 4 – Administration
1. Pick up at printers	1. Deposit check
2. Gather coaching materials	2. Send out cards
3. Finish with students	3. Pay monthly bills online
4. Create timeline/agenda	4. Property legal question
5. Review activity flow/timing	5. Tidy workspace

When we are coaching ourselves to success, we have to constantly ask: *"Is this activity moving me closer to my targeted goal? Is it the most important thing for me to do right now?"*

If the activity is not, then refocus; if the activity is, do it and pat yourself on the back.

YOGA POSTURES AND BREATHING EXERCISES TO ENLIVEN WATER EXPRESSION

These yoga poses will assist the WATER element in reflecting on and enlivening creative impulses for the appropriate expression of emotions. To develop metaphysical awareness in the second energy center, Svadisthana, the following series is useful.

Cobra pose. Resting on your tummy, place your palms flat on the floor directly under the shoulders. Keep your arms and elbows close to the body. Imagine your shoulder blades touch in the back and keep your shoulders down (not lifted toward the ears). Inhale and slide your nose, chin, and chest off the floor using your hands for support. Look up toward the ceiling, thereby stimulating your pituitary and pineal glands. Feel the tension in the back as you tighten your buttocks, keeping your legs straight. Hold the pose until you begin to feel uncomfortable. Exhale and slowly lower your chest, chin, nose, and forehead to the floor. Pause. Repeat three times.

Locust pose. Rest your chin or forehead on the floor and place your fists along the sides of your body close to the groin area. Inhale and lift one leg at a time or both legs at once up toward the ceiling. Keep the top of your hipbone in touch with your arm or floor as much as possible to keep your body from rising off the floor. Hold the pose until you begin to feel uncomfortable. Lower your leg or legs and exhale.

Child's pose. Hinge the buttocks backward onto your bent knees. Rest your head on the floor with your arms stretched out in front and relax. Feel happy and safe as a child in the womb of the mother. Breathe. Relax for thirty seconds or so.

HAND REFLEXOLOGY TO COOL AND BALANCE WATER EXPRESSION

Reflexology of the hands will help you to develop an overall cooling effect on the emotions, support the development of your imagination through reflection, and regain the courage to take your imagination out into the world. Follow the same procedures as described in Chapter 5 (FIRE).

THE MATURE WATER ELEMENT BRINGS REFLECTION AND IMAGINATION

Reflection of life and its mysteries make the WATER element a seeker and a seer of the unseen. An unending supply of divine expression flows from a receptive cup as the imagination leans toward the mystical. When maturely developed, an abundance of creative expression is channeled for transforming negativity through the laws of give-and-take. Cooperation and harmony are keywords as you strive to live a life dedicated to peaceful co-existence.

Step 1. AIR: *"Who am I?"*

Step 2. FIRE: *"What should I do?"*

Step 3. WATER: *"Who and/or what else is involved and how am I feeling about all this?"*

Step 4. EARTH: *"How do I balance the inner and the outer worlds and build a solid foundation on which to stand and move forward?"*

CHAPTER 7

THE EARTH ELEMENT

When we work with the energies of the first chakra, Muladhara, we are dealing with the development of our conscious connection to the planet. Through a sense of order and the use of reason, awareness of the finite material world is provided. The first chakra expression is best described by the EARTH element. Following is an example of a self-expression by an EARTH-preferred person we will call "Bill" in response to a question during coaching to gain greater self-awareness.

The question was the same one asked of Richard (AIR, Chapter 4), Janet (FIRE, Chapter 5), and Danielle (WATER, Chapter 6): *"How would you describe yourself, your strengths, and your gifts, and how you strive to share these with the world?"*

WHAT IS AN EARTH TYPE LIKE?

The EARTH element relates to physical awareness, and manifests through our physical bodies, our feelings of security and safety, and our place on Earth. Bill is a person whose preference is the EARTH element. He always has a solid sense of his place in the world. He enjoys structure and likes order and security. In his words:

"I felt this security through the consistent behaviors that my parents displayed. I came to count on regularity, calmness, quiet, and a congruent sense of where things belonged and how things fit together. I was a child who preferred to think things out before acting on anything. Sometimes I might have thought too long before acting, but I had to sort things out in my mind first before I felt I could move on any thought. Once I had things figured out, I then felt secure in my approach to tackling a project or an assignment. My social side was not very vast; I had few friends as a youth. But although my friends were few in number, I was and still am a loyal friend who attempts to stay connected over the years. There may not be many telephone calls or get-togethers, but there certainly will be the occasional postcard, email, or letter from me. I don't have to hear from others to remember them. I just have a sense of being connected with them.

"I received degrees in mathematics and physics, although I preferred physics to math. I think I took my mathematical mind as far as it wanted to go before I was able to move on to physics as a major. Physics because it explains the physical world to me in a way that I need to understand it, and mathematics because it helps put order in the world around me.

"Some people may find me boring as I don't express my feelings very much. I tend to be a person who goes about my business, seeing what needs to be done, doing it, and being quite content with working on projects where my talents and abilities are useful to others. That does not mean that I can't be creative or sociable, it just means that I may not notice those things that deal with human interactions and may have to be reminded

to do things that others would know naturally to do. Once I do notice or someone reminds me to notice what is socially required by others, then I quite enjoy myself when doing social things and hope that others enjoy being with me.

"Because orderliness means so much to me, I try to honor it when and wherever I can. A demonstration of this was raising our children. I always tried to teach them to put things back where they belonged. The shopping carts at the grocery store belong back in the line-up of carts and not left in the parking lot, for example. When there were candies by the cash register in restaurants, I told them to take one or maybe two, but not a handful. I told them when taking out the garbage to wrap it up carefully and to be sure to take special care of broken glass in it so that the people who have to pick it up will not be hurt. Don't be too loud; never play music so loudly that it would disturb the neighbor's peace and quiet. Shovel the snow from the sidewalk and be sure there is no ice so no one slips. Follow the rules so that there is orderliness for one and all. Do the best job you can at what you are assigned to do. Don't skimp on details or take shortcuts as you'll probably find that if you do, you have made more work for yourself. You may as well take the time to do it right the first time. In thinking this way, you will actually conserve energy in the long run.

"I find that I am willing to do the jobs that others might have little interest in doing, but which give me the satisfaction of completion. My mission on this planet is to ensure that ideas are manifested through tireless and methodical approaches."

HOW TO RECOGNIZE AND DEAL
WITH PITFALLS OF THE EARTH TYPE

Discernment is the gift of the EARTH type. When applying discernment, we need to know how much stability is required in living our lives. When we control the events around us too much, we create tension in our overall inner and outer worlds. Sometimes we have to yield to the tension that strives to destabilize us and learn the lesson that is in front of us. To know how much stability (EARTH) versus instability (WATER because of its fluidity, and FIRE because of its heat and lightness) any system requires or can handle at any given point is the challenge. I once worked with a colleague who started her own business while working as a medical doctor and a director for a walk-in doctor's clinic. She had three children and was married to man with whom she did not get along. I asked her why she didn't leave him and she responded, "Because I just couldn't handle one more thing." If we do not pay attention to the feedback around us, we cannot make responsible adjustments.

If WATER and EARTH can mix well, then EARTH can easily get the feedback it needs to manifest the ideas of AIR with the motivation of FIRE. Unlike the other elements, the EARTH element gets its satisfaction from the actual building of the idea. EARTH may say, *"We have only so much time to produce this idea. I know from past experience that we have to do these measurable steps in this manner for us to get done on time and within budget."*

Sometimes the EARTH element seems to be a "stick-in-the-mud." Having an innate sense of time and space, EARTH often thinks that there is some foolishness in the AIR, FIRE, and WATER elements. EARTH, however, continuously goes about doing its job, getting very little acknowledgment for doing so, but is committed nonetheless to ensuring that the ideas actually are manifested on Earth and within Earth's real time and space limitations.

When hierarchical systems are not dealing with the current needs of people and the resources required to satisfy those needs in appropriate ways, then forces begin to operate to "awaken" the system. In this way, hierarchical systems can continue to evolve rather than be destroyed. As we struggle with our environment to create a stable, secure world, we must at the same time be careful not to become too stuck in this need as instinctual forces will oppose too much stability and will create some chaos by stirring things up.

We can continue to evolve by developing all our capabilities and tapping into the whole system within us: the mind, the emotions, and the body. Carl Jung said the individual ego (AIR-Mental) could be conceived as the commander of a small army in the struggle with his environment (WATER-Social), a war not infrequently on two fronts: ahead, the outer struggle for existence (EARTH-Physical); and in the rear, the internal struggle against rebellious instinctual nature (FIRE-Social).[8]

When dealing with our place on Earth, the personality is dealing with its relationship to the opposing forces of fear versus safety, or how secure we feel with others in the world. When issues around security are not dealt with, we will continue to be offered opportunities for breakthrough, breakdown, or breaking with "the old."

Our work with the EARTH element also addresses our connections to our original family and their authority over us. Emotions may surface that relate to our fear of not getting fair treatment. Lacking trust in people leads us to need to over-control. If, on the other hand, we feel too secure in our world, we tend to get complacent. Here we expect that things are the way we think they should be because that is the way they have always been. We become too set in our ways and reduce our ability to be flexible and adaptable to an ever-changing world.

I recall one engineering firm that I did some training for about twenty years ago when the old established firms had the lead in their industries just because they were established and had longstanding recognition of being good at what they did. However, times were

---

8   Jung, C.G. *Psychology and Religion*. New York: Yale University Press. 1938.

changing: More engineering firms were showing up, and now not only did the companies have to be technically good, but customer service and friendliness were becoming just as important—even more important— than historical reputation. In other words, clients were demanding not just technical competency, but friendly, fast, and fair service.

We tend to gravitate to occupations that suit our natural tendencies. Engineering is an occupation that draws on mechanical skills and "constructive" methods, and that traditionally does not require the honing of social skills—unlike, for example, an occupation in sales, which requires a high degree of social-skills development. One engineer said to me that he felt that taking customers out to lunch was like "kissing ass." He did not approve of it, nor did he enjoy it.

I showed the group of about one hundred engineers how their personality profiles compared with statistics on typical profiles of engineers. Their profiles matched and fell into the same categories: first preference, physical; second preference, mental; and least preference, social. No one was surprised, and many felt that the social side was not all that important and in some ways childish. The president, however, said that the information I had shared was exactly what he was looking for, and in his closing remarks to the group addressed the subject of complacency. His basic message was: *"We cannot stand on past laurels. Times have changed, and complacency is the worst inner sense to have because it prevents you from learning, growing, striving, and ultimately evolving."*

To develop discernment, we need to confront our fears. Ask yourself: *"What are the things I am afraid of?"* By bringing our fears to the surface, we can look at them and gather the feedback required to address them responsibly. You then can ask yourself: *"What can I do to address my fears and achieve a secure place in the world while nurturing and protecting the resources of my community?"*

HOW TO RECOGNIZE "EARTH" MOMENTS WHEN EARTH IS NOT YOUR NATURAL PREFERENCE

When EARTH is not your natural preference and is undeveloped or unfamiliar, it can take on inappropriate expressions. It can be expressed as overly controlling or overly parental. For example, when working with others to get a job done, you over- emphasize the importance of the work at the expense of the personal relationships. Another expression might be an over-reaction to a fear. For example, afraid that others are "out to get you," you sabotage the group. In this case, it's your fear about trust and security that is coming to the surface. Whereas in the past you may have gone to discuss things, you now find other and perhaps covert ways to satisfy your needs. In these types of instances, people will very likely say that you are not "acting like yourself."

COACHING TOOLS TO ENLIVEN PHYSICAL AWARENESS

In the movie *Jerry Maguire*, Jerry collates and hands out his "dream" to his colleagues, then later as he finds only scenes and images of war on television, he suddenly realizes and regrets what he has done. He is embarrassed by his "dream" and having exposed it, and he feels that he has made a fool of himself with his colleagues.

Jerry's inner Critic spoke up—just as what happens to us when we imagine and think of a dream or a vision for ourselves. We all can hear that voice of our inner Critic:

- *"You can't have that because you're not good enough."*
- *"Who do you think you are anyway to even imagine you could have that?"*
- *"What happens when you fail again? What will everyone think?"*

- *"You're such a goodie-two-shoes and always do what you're supposed to do, not what you want to do."*

On and on goes the Critic in us as it starts to wear us down, diminish our enthusiasm, and undermine our confidence. When coaching yourself to wellness, it is best to take the bull by the horns and invite in the Critic rather than ignore or resist it. This is a very powerful method for working with the EARTH element (and one of my most important coaching tips to share with others).

LET THE CRITIC SPEAK. This exercise is adapted from some techniques I was introduced to years ago. Rate each of the following statements on a scale of 1 (lowest) to 5 (highest) in terms of your confidence in being able to sustain your efforts over the long haul.

- The dream/goal is desirable and worth living/achieving.
    1   2   3   4   5
- The dream/goal is possible for me to live/achieve all of the time.
    1   2   3   4   5
- What I have to do to live/achieve the dream/goal is appropriate for me in my life right now.
    1   2   3   4   5
- I have the capabilities necessary to live/achieve the dream/goal.
    1   2   3   4   5
- I deserve to live/achieve the dream/goal and carry it forward.
    1   2   3   4   5

What typically happens in a coaching session is that each statement is given a high rating. I will say:

"I see that the ratings are all high, so there must not be a problem in living/achieving this dream/goal. If there is no problem, why have you not lived/achieved this dream/goal in the past?"

Then, I ask for the statements to be reviewed and rated again with this perspective in mind to see what surfaces. Do the same yourself to find what surfaces for you.

For example, you might begin to wonder if it is really possible to live/achieve your dream/goal: *"I still have a whole lot of that 'little-girl' stuff in me that inhibits me from wanting to play a bigger game on planet Earth. I certainly didn't have role models to draw on when I grew up in my one-company 'Leave-it-to-Beaver' town in the fifties where we were all taught to conform to the status quo."*

Flushing out the Critic's voice will help you to move forward on your dream/goal. For example: *"Now that I acknowledge that 'little girl' in me, I can see and consciously address what may block or sabotage me as I move toward my dream/goal. Being more aware of this possibility allows me to make better, more mature decisions on what I want to do to move forward. If I am not conscious of what may block or sabotage me, I am limited in my choices. So I want to become as conscious as possible with the inner workings of my mind to expand my abilities to make choices."*

Continue to invite in the Critic—without second-guessing or censoring yourself. Let it all come out.

- If I live/achieve this dream/goal, then …

  _____

- It is not possible for me to live/achieve this dream/goal because …

  _____

- I am not capable of living/achieving this dream/goal because …

  _____

- It is wrong for me to want to live/achieve this dream/goal because ...

  _____

- I don't deserve to live/achieve this dream/goal because ...

  _____

- Other negative beliefs I have:

  _____

The Critic is designed and intends to protect us, but sometimes it overprotects us and prevents us from moving forward. In managing the Critic, we can address obstacles and turn them into action items; or, perhaps we simply need to honor its voice and slow down our process until we are stronger, more ready, have more resources, or whatever. There may be an inner ecological necessity for holding back. Explore and challenge the Critic. Flush it out. What is it trying to say? Pay attention.

We honor the Critic by hearing and respecting its voice, and in so doing it helps us in furthering our AIR-Dreamer work. Now the Critic is at the level of our consciousness, and having it there will give us power and energy to move forward. The Critic is to be valued: Its purpose always has been and is to protect us.

POST-IT NOTES. Keep working with the Critic in you and allow yourself to ride the waves it shares. Make a post-it note for each "voice" about why you cannot live/achieve your dream/goal. You may end up with ten or twenty post-it notes to stick on a wall or a flipchart to review and arrange into groups—very likely you will find they are easy to place into three or four general categories. Arrange the post-it notes by categories, then label each category with a post-it note.

As we explore our beliefs around why we cannot live/achieve our dream/goal, we can pinpoint the obstacles that will confront us on our journey and turn these obstacles into steppingstones. Here is an example of the obstacles flushed out by someone we will call "Elaine".

1. *Who do you think you are?*
2. *We don't draw attention to ourselves.*
3. *We suffer; that's more our style.*
4. *You're such a "goodie-two-shoes" immature and unsophisticated person.*
5. *What will everyone say when you fail?*

Two main obstacles that Elaine identified centered on "judgments of others" and "you can't call it work if you're not suffering." These internal voices, designed to serve Elaine in some way, came mainly from her mother and her grandmother, both of whom she said loved her in their way. These were internal programs she carried around within herself that were now outdated, but still driving her life and her choices, and ultimately her results.

Elaine actually is a mature, sophisticated woman who knows herself, but she needed to reprogram herself to learn that failure is nothing but feedback. In guiding her through further exploration of the Critic in her and its voices, her fears around failure diminished.

We started with the questions:

- *Failure according to whom?*
- *Failure according to what?*

As we worked, Elaine began to understand the Critic in her and from whom and where its voices came. With this greater awareness, she recognized that she had the opportunity to make a more conscious choice about who was running her life. She could take charge of her own life and find ways to alter the internal programs she carried around within herself. She began to realize that she was the main player in the show and drama of her life and that everyone else was just a bit player. She began to learn that she could develop her own personal voice and speak about what was important to her.

We want to use to our advantage the Critic in us and the gift of EARTH's detailed approach, which strives to conserve energy and protect us by not undertaking unnecessary actions before first getting all of the detailed information required. Now that we have more information, we can start to create some action items, turning obstacles into steppingstones.

It is the FIRE-Realist (Social-Mental) in us that turns obstacles into steppingstones and ultimately into action items. The FIRE-Realist does not see obstacles; it sees only actions and steps to take. If, for example, I were to decide that I will swim to lose weight, the EARTH-Critic in me might say: "You can't go swimming; you don't even own a bathing suit!" The FIRE-Realist in me would simply encourage me to beg, borrow, or steal a bathing suit if I need one.

Here is how the FIRE-Realist in Elaine responded to her obstacles once they were surfaced:

1. *Who do you think you are?*

   FIRE-Realist: You'll find out who you are as you move in the direction of your dream/goal.

   - P/T studies
   - Exercise – swimming 2x / week; go with neighbor
   - Rebounding – 2x / day @ 2 min
   - Circulatory mat work – 2x / day @ 2 min
   - Walk lake road and commune with nature – 3x / wk

2. *We don't draw attention to ourselves.*

   FIRE-Realist: Look for ways to draw attention to yourself so that you can develop greater confidence along the way.

   • Do more in-class presentations
   • Speak own mind in discussions

3. *We suffer; that's more our style.*

   FIRE-Realist: When you suffer, use that as feedback that it is time to please and enjoy yourself. We were put on this planet to increase and enliven happiness and joy. Suffering feelings are indicators that you need to find ways to experience happiness and joy.

   • Take more time for reading
   • Give self permission to have fun—re-create in your adult mind that your mother and grandmother give you their permission and also wish they had done so for themselves
   • Take more walks in nature

4. *You're such a "goodie-two-shoes" immature and unsophisticated person.*

   FIRE-Realist: Thank you for sharing.

5. *What will everyone say when you fail?*

   FIRE-Realist: There is no such thing as failure, only feedback. Others can think and say what they like as that is *their* process; *yours* is to live your life through your own intentions.

YOGA POSTURES AND BREATHING EXERCISES TO ENLIVEN EARTH EXPRESSION

These yoga poses will assist the EARTH element to deal with fears and to develop discernment at the metaphysical base chakra, Muladhara.

1. Sit in a comfortable, stable position with the spine straight, your hands resting on your knees and your eyes closed. Begin the journey into a meditative state by focusing on your breathing. The mind needs somewhere to place its attention for it to cooperate with the process of meditation. You will notice thoughts: Notice and do not do anything. Just notice.

2. Continue to focus on your breathing. Without attention to any end result, sit silently in this manner for ten to fifteen minutes.

3. Preparing to come out of the meditative state, slowly and gently register awareness of your body and how it is sitting in the upright position.

4. Now, lie down for two minutes, registering the peace and silence you felt in meditation before going back into activity. Take this peace with you and return to this meditative state at your next sitting.

Once in the morning and once in the evening is all you need to begin to feel the connection of your physical self with your spiritual self, that self which is connected to the spiritual realm of all possibilities.

FOOT REFLEXOLOGY TO STIMULATE AND GROUND EARTH EXPRESSION

Reflexology of the feet will help to facilitate a stimulating, yet grounding effect in your body. Your use of discernment that is more grounded will assist you to regain the appropriate way to care for others through diligent completion of tasks.

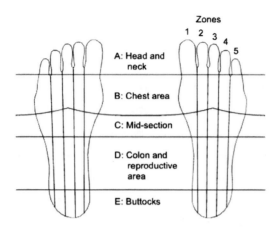

Zones
1 2 3 4 5

A: Head and neck

B: Chest area

C: Mid-section

D: Colon and reproductive area

E: Buttocks

1. Warm-up. Start by rubbing your hands together, generating warmth. Sit on the floor or on a comfortable chair. Bend the right knee so that you can place your right foot on your left thigh area with the sole (plantar side) of your foot facing you. Rub and wring the foot as if trying to squeeze out something. This stimulates circulation.

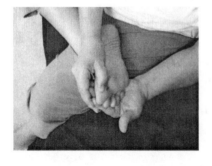

2. A – Relax tension in reflexes related to head, neck, eyes, and ears. Hold your right foot with your left hand, the fingers supporting the toes behind and your right fingers under them for stability. Starting at the big toe, press your right or left thumb (you may alternate) into the pad, giving it a pressure point massage. Then, slowly thumb-walk (apply your thumb in a press-release manner) from the base to the top of the pad. Work each toe three times.

3. Webs – Relax tension in reflexes related to neck and shoulder area. Massage and tug the webs between the toes.

4. B – Relax tension in reflexes related to chest, breast, and lung areas.
Grasp the right foot with your left thumb on the plantar side and your
left fingers behind. Starting where sections B and C meet, thumb-walk
upward between the valleys of the (metatarsal) bones. Work all four
valleys three times.

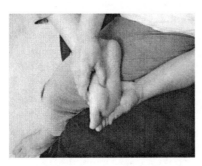

5. C – Relax tension in reflexes
related to stomach, liver,
pancreas, and spleen areas.
Thumb-walk section C, working
the entire area thoroughly three
times.

6. D – Relax tension in reflexes related to colon and reproductive system.
Thumb-walk section D, working the entire area thoroughly three times.
(If your thumb gets tired, you may use the other thumb.)

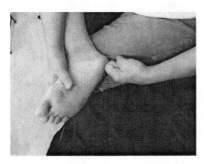

7. E – Relax tension in reflexes
related to buttocks area.
Supporting the foot with your
right hand, use the knuckle of
your left index finger to apply
a pressure point massage to the
U-shaped area of the heel.

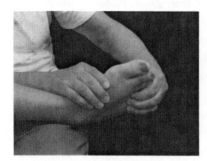

8. Top of foot (dorsal) – Relax tension in reflexes related to back area. Using both hands, place your thumbs on the plantar side of the foot and wrap your fingers around the top of the foot. Press and release your index finger along the valleys between the (metatarsal) bones, working from the base of the toes toward the ankle area. (You may alternate between index fingers.) Repeat three times.

9. Ankle – Relax tension in reflexes related to groin-lymphatic area. With your left middle finger, press and release along the indentation from one ankle bone to the other. Repeat three times.

10. Lateral side of foot – Relax tension in reflexes related to peripheral areas such as arms, hips, and legs. Grab the flesh on the outer edge of the foot at the base of the baby toe, your thumb on the plantar side and your fingers on the top side. Use a pinch-and-release motion to work toward the heel, covering zone 5 thoroughly.

11. Medial side of foot – Relax tension in reflexes related to spine area. Thumb-walk along the medial side of zone 1 from the heel to the top of the big toe. Slide the thumb back down to the heel and repeat three times.

12. Conclusion. Rub and stroke your foot as you did when you started. Repeat the entire procedure on your left foot. After completing both feet, massage them with lotion. Pause and end your session with a couple of deep breaths, inhaling through your nose and exhaling slowly through your mouth. Feel the effects of this circulatory work throughout your body. Notice the stimulating and grounding effects throughout your whole system.

FEET MASSAGE MAT. A wonderful self-help tool for stimulating reflexes in the feet between treatments is the massage mat. Wear socks when first using the massage mat and whenever your feet feel tender.

Following is a one-minute round of six exercises to do twice each session. Do two sessions per day, one in the morning and one in the evening.

Place the massage mat flat on the floor next to the back of a chair. Step onto the mat and hold the back of the chair for support, then march your feet up and down to a count of ten for each position:

1. ... on the flats;   2. ... on the toes;

3. ... on the outsides;

4. ... on the heels;

5. ... on the insteps;

6. ... again on the flats.

THE MATURE EARTH ELEMENT BRINGS DISCERNMENT

The solid and stable energy of the EARTH element ensures the production of our wealth and our sense of security. Wealth and security are vital to a peaceful and happy life. EARTH people are methodical, thrifty, and practical. They responsibly use grounded energy in their slow and steady progress to acquire stability and security. When balanced, work and leisure go hand in hand. Mature EARTH people respect and value the material world by appreciating the need for conservation and the wise use of resources. They hold a deep concern for the welfare of the community and the planet.

This completes the system of elements and their use—nature's gift to us:

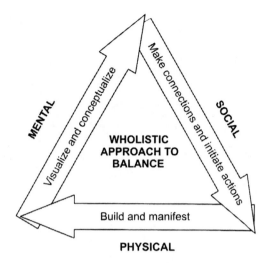

We need self-awareness, objective frameworks for processing our information, and understanding of our actions and their impact on our lives. And we need to feel balanced and enjoy life—something that only we can achieve for ourselves. We require hardiness and flexibility, and we need to be resilient: Life is a gift, but it also is a challenge—this is how we grow!

PART III

PURSUIT OF A
WELL-TEMPERED LIFE

The journey toward a well-tempered life is never over. Life goes on, and there is always something to learn. Having tools such as the ones presented in this book available to us can help to keep us on an even keel. The tools in this book have certainly helped me. I hope they help you, too.

Tempered: possessing both the hardiness
and the flexibility needed to be resilient

CHAPTER **8**

MY PERSONAL JOURNEY

My journey in pursuit of a well-tempered life began in earnest after the death of my first husband when I was twenty-seven. It is common for people to question what life means after a traumatic event, and this was so for me. My journey has included so much valuable learning from wonderful teachers to whom I am eternally grateful.

I began with meditation. When I started practicing meditation, I felt like I had come home. Meditation seemed so natural for me and gave me feelings of peace. These feelings made me hungry to understand more and I decided to take a year-long course on yoga training for instructors.

During that year, one of my teachers introduced me to Vita-Flex, which is a pressure point therapy method similar to reflexology. I was amazed by what Vita-Flex could do. I was experiencing menstrual cramps when my teacher demonstrated some pressure points on me. Through his pressure point work, my cramps dissipated. I couldn't believe it. I was used to taking pain relievers, and now through pressure point work my body could heal itself on its own.

At about this time, my son was diagnosed with a curvature of his spine. X-rays showed that because of incorrect positioning of one leg into the hip socket, the cause of the curvature of the spine, one leg was about a half inch shorter than the other leg.

During my Vita-Flex training, I asked my teacher if the technique could lengthen a leg. I was being a bit facetious when I asked, but he said that there were leg-lengthening points in the collarbone area, and that if I brought in my son, he would show me the points to work, which would need to be done for about three months to correct the condition.

I worked these points on my son every morning before he went school. This set of pressure points took me about two minutes to do, and after three months, we went for more X-rays. To everyone's amazement, the problem was no longer there; the leg and spine were completely normalized—"remission" the doctors called it. I asked the doctors what they would have done to correct the problem, and they said they would have shaved some bone off one foot and put a lift in the shoe of the other foot. In their minds, this would have corrected the imbalance.

It would have been a mechanical correction; it would not have been a natural healing. This is when I fully realized and accepted the power of the natural healing arts, and knew I needed to learn more about them. When we do not know that there are alternative and complementary ways of doing things, we use only one frame of reference to make decisions and we are limited by the restrictions that frame our experience.

Over the next few years, I took every natural healing arts course I could find. I became certified in teaching yoga, reflexology, iridology, deep reflexology therapy massage, attunements ... you name it, I enlisted.

There was so much very exciting "new-age" stuff happening in the seventies. I couldn't and didn't keep up with everything; there was simply too much. However, I did and continue to work with personality theory, reflexology, and yoga. And there are a number of people who merit special acknowledgment and I wish to credit for the work I do.

Dr. Ramamurti S. Mishra, my spiritual teacher, taught many lessons about life and yoga. I learned how to use sound for meditation and spiritual healing. I learned to see life as a drama that provided opportunities for spiritual growth. I learned to engage in yoga and how yoga can heal and help, especially during times of struggle. I learned about the yoga chakra energy centers of consciousness and how these centers have positive and negative attributes.

My degree and interest in psychology took me to the wonderful knowledge of the Myers-Briggs Type Indicator® (MBTI®). My certification has helped me to learn and understand more about "people differences." The MBTI®, drawn from the work of Dr. Carl G. Jung and developed by Katherine Briggs and Isobel Myers, became a basis for the extensive reading that I adored throughout my years of studying as a student and apprentice.

What I began to notice was that the gifts and struggles that came out of the functions and processes first described by Jung were very similar to the gifts and struggles identified in the four lower yoga chakras.

My studies in psychology also included the works of Abraham Maslow and his definition of life's struggles based on a hierarchy of needs. Again I could see that the struggles to evolve through satisfying our needs were similar to the struggles recognized by Jung and in yoga.

I relate the four basic human needs described by Maslow to the four elements and the yoga chakra system:

1. **Security** – which Maslow says has to be satisfied before affiliation. Survival and security needs, represented in the base chakra Muladhara, correspond to the element of EARTH. This is about the material world, the world where we build the tangible manifestations of our ideas—the world of measurement.

2. **Affiliation** – which Maslow says has to be satisfied after security and before power. Affiliation is represented in the second chakra, Svadisthana, which corresponds to the element of WATER. This is about adaptability, fluidity, cooperation, blending, connecting, and harmonizing.

3. **Power or Will** – which Maslow says has to be satisfied after affiliation and before self-actualizing. Power or will, represented by the third chakra, Manipura, corresponds to the element of FIRE. This is about expressing ourselves, connecting actions to ideas, confronting challenges, and being recognized for our individuality.

4. **Self-Actualization** – which Maslow says has to be satisfied after power or will, and is represented by the heart chakra, Anahata, which corresponds to the element of AIR. This is about learning, growing, exploring, evolving, mentoring, and inventing.

My quest for knowledge included Neurolinguistic Programming (NLP), which I studied with Robert Dilts. He taught how to explore the cognitive interpretations of the thinking mind. The thinking mind creates neural pathways based on language that ultimately creates the programming in the mind of the meaning we give to our lives. Our interpretations of events in our lives, based on pain or pleasure responses, can be revealed through questions. For example, we may be making current decisions about our life based on an event that happened when we were five years old. We interpreted that event in some way that may be influencing our decisions today. The problem is that we have most likely outlived the value of a five-year-old child's interpretation of an event long ago on a fifty-year-old adult's decisions now.

In NLP we explore the content the mind is using, which is often limited by earlier programming. When we explore it, we expand our conscious awareness of the content as well as expand our possibilities for choices to deal with it. If we do not explore the content, we stay limited in our options and we fail to see creative solutions to problems, even though alternative solutions might be right in front of us.

Let's do an exercise: What number is most different from the others? Circle your choice.

1) One   2) Thirteen   3) Thirty-One

How many choices do you think you have? Three? Or six? Most people think there are three choices: the three spelled-out numbers. Few people see there are actually six choices: the three spelled-out numbers and the three numerals.

For me, the number that is most different from the others is "2"—which most people fail to even consider as a choice.

The mind makes assumptions, and in so doing fails to see the entirety of what is actually "there" and what might be the most "logical" choice. Most people filter out the three numerals as choices and therefore fail to consider "2" as a possible answer—the choice that doesn't include either "one" or "1" or "three" or "3".

Throughout my career in professional and personal training and development, I have worked with all of these tools and insights from my many years of study. For example, I apply Elemental Personality Theory (EPT) in corporate team-building, management coaching, couple's problem-solving, and one-on-one personal coaching. I combine the four elements for identifying individual struggles with problem-solving processes. Through a facilitative process of questioning about a problem related to a job, a manager, or a colleague, or to a spouse, a child, or an in-law, people can clarify their problem and expand their possibilities for creative solutions; they can step outside their frame of reference to see alternatives—consider the "2" as in the example of in the exercise.

PROBLEM-SOLVING. Following is the basic sequence of coaching phases that I find works best once a problem has been identified and defined:

- First, ask the mind what kind of goal or outcome it is after in order to solve the problem. This phase calls for our use of the AIR-Dreamer's mental awareness in us.
- Next, address the EARTH-Critic's physical awareness to identify the obstacles to achieving the goal or outcome. This phase helps to surface what we perceive as "in the way" of getting to the goal or outcome, the obstacles we will need to deal with in order to move forward.
- Once we are aware of the obstacles, we can then bring in the social-mental awareness of the FIRE-Realist to turn the obstacles into steppingstones, or action items. Applying our will or the force of our focused power, we take action to move forward and begin to solve the problem.
- Finally, we go to the social-physical awareness of the WATER-Catalyst to make connections to the people and resources needed to close the gap between current reality and the future goal or outcome. Who and what can we enlist or ask for support in moving toward the goal or outcome?

Here is an example of my self-coaching process in a situation that was causing a lot of stress and tension:

A client had given me checks that were not cashable due to insufficient funds in her account. I tried to work with her on ways to resolve her debt with me, but I eventually realized that she was a scam artist and stringing me along.

At first I was angry, which is a normal response, but once I accepted the reality of the situation, I quickly realized that she held emotional power over me unless I could come to terms with the situation. I asked myself what was the real reason for my elevated stress and tension, and in searching for the answer, I realized that it was actually more about concern for the money we needed to pay for our mounting renovation bills.

The stress and tension originally was about being a victim in someone's scam, but once I accepted that I had been scammed, the problem became about how to pay our bills. So, I called our bank manager and got an extension on our line of credit until I could deal with the scamming—which I eventually did through small-claims court and won.

This is how I applied the phases of problem-solving to my situation:

Problem: Stress over how to pay bills.

AIR-Dreamer: Outcome. My AIR-Dreamer defined the outcome to the problem as: *"My bills are paid and I am relaxed."*

EARTH-Critic: Obstacles. My EARTH-Critic defined why I could not have this outcome as: *"I don't have enough money to pay my bills."*

FIRE-Realist: Actions. My FIRE-Realist defined the actions to take as: *"Find more money."*

WATER-Catalyst: Connections. My WATER-Catalyst defined the connections to make as: *"Talk to the bank manager and find out what can be done by the bank."*

Solution: The bank manager extends our line of credit and we pay our bills.

Notice that the situation of the scamming was not resolved, but was defined as another problem. It is important when coaching—yourself or others—to work systematically and logically, to "chunk down" and focus on one problem or outcome at a time.

PROCESS WORKSHEET. The life-coaching process outlined here can be followed to work systematically on a problem of yours or someone else and move forward toward achieving a goal or outcome.

A problem is defined as the gap between the current reality and a goal or outcome. By flushing out the components of the problem, we can use our holistic system to create a new way of being in our world and close the gap between our current reality and our goal or outcome.

Step 1: Identification of Problem

What is the problem?

_____

Step 2: The First Phase – AIR-Dreamer-Mental

If you could have it the way you really want it, how would that be?

_____

Step 3: The Second Phase – EARTH-Critic-Physical

What stops you from being able to achieve your goal or outcome?

Obstacle 1: _____

Obstacle 2: _____

Obstacle 3: _____

Step 4: The Third Phase – FIRE-Realist-Social

What actions do you need to take to overcome the obstacles and achieve your goal or outcome?

_____

_____

Step 5: The Fourth Phase – WATER-Catalyst-Social
What resources (people or things) do you need to draw on to overcome these obstacles and achieve your goal or outcome?

_____

_____

Step 6: Timeline of Goal or Outcome
By what date can you reasonably expect to have undertaken each action item that you have identified as necessary to overcome obstacles and achieve your goal or outcome?

_____

_____

CLOSING REMARKS. For some thirty years, I have taught classes and workshops in yoga, reflexology, and elemental personality theory. I continue to work with and apply the insights and tools of these disciplines with clients, family, friends, and myself to deal with situations that cause imbalances in our mental awareness, social awareness, and physical awareness. These imbalances caused by stressful situations can diminish our health and well-being, and the best prevention is to stay awake, alert, and aware. We can never be aware enough. Life often throws us curves and if we can anticipate them, we have a better chance of dealing with them and maintaining our well-being, our wellness, and our happiness.

As a not-so-untypical individual who struggles from time to time over differences with people, stressful situations, physical challenges of the body, and pressures imposed by the mind, I've learned that the tools we can draw on for dealing with these struggles are the very tools that can cause the struggles: the four lower chakras. Once I become aware of a struggle, I strive to work with it in a conscious way, using every opportunity that life offers to teach me more about my own awakening self.

An important thing to remember is that desires are always present. These desires, like nature itself, always seek manifestation. Be sure to desire positive, creative, and productive things. Do not do things to "not die;" do things to enjoy living—as a by-product, you will not die.

Analyze stressful situations and find alternative approaches, goals, or strategies once you are more aware of how these situations are affecting you. Become a learner of life and continuously ask what you can learn from every situation. Life is the meaningful co-existence of opposite values. We cannot know one value without experiencing the opposite. A person blind from birth cannot know what darkness is because they have never known light.

According to Dr. Carl Jung, the father of personality typology, the tension of opposites is the very essence of life itself. Without tension, there would be no energy and consequently no personality distinctions—we would all be the same! We cannot appreciate happiness without experiencing unhappiness. We cannot appreciate safety without understanding and knowing about fear. Even with fear comes information. The bottom line is that we cannot understand ourselves without bumping up against the differences in how others think, feel, and do things. This is how we grow. This is how we temper our skills in life. Through life itself, we can become stronger with every interaction. This makes life very dynamic and very exciting: Everything that happens is really only feedback. And what we do with this feedback is strictly up to us!

With information and self awareness, we can make better decisions on how to proceed in any situation. With a love of life as the basis within, strive at all times for productive, creative outcomes with others. As world-renowned chiropractor Dr. Bernard Jensen, a pioneer of research on longevity, has said: *"I'm going to love you whether you want me to or not because it is good for me."*

It is our choice to use tension to create either growth and integration or shattering and disintegration in our lives. The challenge is to use our minds to constantly bring ourselves back to the union of opposites, back into balance. We will always and forever be pulled in many directions as our desires strive to be manifested—this is simply the nature of life.

We all wish for a life that is full of creative and productive results that stimulate internal joy, happiness, and well-being for ourselves. When we achieve balance, internal joy, and feelings of happiness for ourselves, others will naturally be touched and benefit.

Develop self-awareness, stay positive, maintain yourself as the locus of control in your life, and take care of yourself along the way. In so doing, you will be amazed at how situations around you improve!

I believe that we have to develop and strengthen the four lower chakras to support a stable spiritual side for ourselves—a life that has purpose, meaning, and vision. This growth takes place over our lifetime. As long as we have a body, we will have struggles. As long as we have struggles, we have opportunities to expand our consciousness and learn more about ourselves. I don't go looking for problems, but when they find me, I don't avoid them. In this way, I strive to lead a well-tempered life—a life that is tempered by life itself. There is always more to learn about ourselves, and whether we like it or not, life—or shit, as some say—happens.

We are each bodies of energy in a physical body, and any work on self-awareness is good work that can assist us in gaining clarity, direction, and purpose in our lives and in the legacy we want to leave behind. What is the legacy you want to leave behind? What will people say about you at your funeral? Do you want to leave a lasting legacy of what you want to be remembered for? Think about it, and as Brendon Burchard says in his Expert Academy trainings, commit to doing it now! What else are you going to be doing in the next eighteen months?

Life is too short to waste, and it is too precious to hold back on out of fear of failure—or of anything else. What I tell people who claim they want to hold back is to at least do it consciously. And actually, there is no such thing as failure—only feedback and things to learn about our choices.

The aim of yoga is to consciously apply life's forces within us— the forces that can be represented by the four elements of AIR, FIRE, WATER, and EARTH, which strive to be expressed maturely to satisfy our needs and desires—to integrate and yoke the mind, body, and spirit together with the two forces of the invisible and the visible.

THE INVISIBLE EMPOWERS THE VISIBLE REALITY

HUMAN-VISIBLE	BEING-INVISIBLE
Mind and Body	Love and Truth
Relative World	Spiritual World
Four lower chakras	Three higher chakras

Desires are natural and healthy, but how we go about satisfying them is a question we must ask ourselves: We are interdependent with one another, and we together must take care of the entire planet if we individually wish to survive.

Apply wisely your four elements of AIR, FIRE, WATER, and EARTH—tools to develop and express maturely within the "human," or relative, world while tapping into and drawing on the qualities of love and truth within the "being" of the spiritual world; tools to create a world worth living and enjoy the greatest gift of all: life itself.

Tempered: possessing both the hardiness
and the flexibility needed to be resilient

ANCIENT SANSKRIT POEM
— Author Unknown

Look to this day, for it is life
The very life of life.
In its brief course
Lie all the realities and truths of existence.
The joy of growth, the splendor of action,
The glory of power.
For yesterday is but a memory, and
Tomorrow is only a vision, but today well lived
Makes every yesterday a memory of happiness
And every tomorrow a vision of hope.
Look well therefore to this day.

APPENDIX

PERSONAL SOUL PSYCHOLOGY FRAMEWORK

ELEMENT / CHAKRA	AWARENESS / FUNCTION	MOVEMENT / TENSE	BALANCED / IMBALANCED
AIR	Mental	Upward	Balanced
IDEAS – Aspect of our thinking mind that draws on the infinite source from above— the over-mind or super-consciousness. Chakra: **Anahata** Gift: *ATTENTION*	Represents INTELLECT. Provides sight and overview. **Dreamer** Higher purpose is insight, and it serves in seeing the world from a clear perspective. Archetype of the FATHER, initiator of ideas, creator of new concepts and inventions.	Movement of this energy is upward and spacious. **Future** Oriented to the future or interplanetary time rather than to Earth time.	Attention of mature Dreamer provides us with our sense of identity, and gives us focus, clarity, and compassion. **Imbalanced** Immature Dreamer is detached from the world, becomes confused, and flits from idea to idea, seeming intolerant of others.

ELEMENT / CHAKRA	AWARENESS / FUNCTION	MOVEMENT / TENSE	BALANCED / IMBALANCED
FIRE ACTIONS – Aspect of our subconscious mind that provides link to the thinking mind and its suggestions. Sets out to turn ideas into realities in a progressive forward-moving way. Chakra: **Manipura** Gift: *VIGILANCE*	Social-Mental Represents WILL or POWER. Connects our social awareness to our mental awareness and activates ideas through actions. **Realist** Higher purpose is to light the way for others, and it functions to show us what next to do. Archetype of the WARRIOR. Goes against conventional ways and sees only what is directly ahead. Acts as if all ideas are achievable, providing new ways to do things.	Outward and upward Movement of this energy is outward and upward as it evaporates water through the heat of combustion. **Present** Operates in the present in trial-and-error way, with strong emphasis on immediate requirements to bring ideas forward.	Balanced Intuition of mature Realist illuminates the way for others to follow. **Imbalanced** Immature Realist becomes self-absorbed and uses up resources without replenishing them. Not learning from the past, it burns up everything in its way, feels frustrated, and frustrates others. As if suspended in space, it fails to "build down" due to its many gains and losses along the way.

ELEMENT / CHAKRA	AWARENESS / FUNCTION	MOVEMENT / TENSE	BALANCED / IMBALANCED
WATER REACTIONS – Aspect of the subconscious mind that responds to AIR and FIRE, causing a catalytic reaction of expansion and growth. Links us to the conscious mind in the physical EARTH element. Chakra: **Svadis** Gift: *REFLECTION*	Social-Physical Represents IMAGINATION. Provides our reactions to ideas of the Dreamer and actions of the Realist. Connects our social awareness to our physical awareness through feelings and emotions. **Catalyst** Higher purpose is to empower, and it functions to surface emotions. Archetype of the JUDGE. Surfaces emotions, resolves differences, and mediates tensions of ideas, actions, and feelings to come up with new ways of processing things.	Outward and downward Movement of this energy is outward and downward, assisting EARTH to become less solid by surfacing things to be dealt with through a cause-and-effect process. **Past, present, and future** Has an organic sense of time, moving through the past, the present, and the future in a non-linear fashion.	Balanced Reflections on feelings of mature Catalyst harmonizes and brings people together, acting as our social conscience as it surfaces unconscious patterns for integration into the conscious mind. Imbalanced Immature Catalyst lacks its own form and a personal sense of self. Feelings of despair are experienced along with a murky sense of integrity.

ELEMENT / CHAKRA	AWARENESS / FUNCTION	MOVEMENT / TENSE	BALANCED / IMBALANCED
EARTH	Physical	Downward	Balanced
FORMATION – Aspect of our conscious existence that through its sense of order and use of reason provides us with awareness of the fintie material world Chakra: **Muladhar** Gift: *DISCERNMENT*	Represents the BODY. Provides us with structure, form, and feedback. **Critic** Higher purpose is to nurture everyone and everything, and it functions by telling us what is missing. Archetype of the MOTHER. As a receptor, holds and nurtures ideas of AIR, actions of FIRE, and reactions of WATER.	Movement of this energy is downward as it solidifies ideas into tangibles by drawing on wisdoms of past. **Past** Focuses on previous experiences to find gaps in the present, and tries to modify our processes to ensure formation and manifestation of our ideas.	Wisdom of mature Critic acts as a stabilizing force for ensuring responsible wealth and security are manifested. **Imbalanced** Due to feeling isolated and unappreciated, immature Critic causes chaos through destructive patterns that destabilize.

Recommended Readings

Burroughs, S. *Healing for the Age of Enlightenment*. Hawaii: Stanley
Burroughs. 1976.

Campbell, Joseph (Ed.). *The Portable Jung*. U.S.: The Viking Press. 1978.

Jung, C.G. *Memories, Dreams, Reflections*. New York: Vintage Books. 1965.

Kroeger, O. & J.M. Thuesen. *Type Talk*. New York: Dell Publishing. 1988.

Kushi, M. *How to See Your Health: Book of Oriental Diagnosis*. Tokyo: Japan
Publications, Inc. 1980.

Progoff, I. *Jung's Psychology and Its Social Meaning*. New York: Anchor Press /
Doubleday. 1973.

SPECIAL RECOGNITION TO MY YOGA TEACHER

Shri Brahmananda Sarasvati (Ramamurti S. Mishra, M.D.).
Fundamentals of Yoga. Monroe, NY: Baba Bhagavandas Publication
Trust. 2002.

Shri Brahmananda Sarasvati (Ramamurti S. Mishra, M.D.). *Pulsation
of Godhood*. Monroe, NY: Baba Bhagavandas Publication Trust.
2001.

Shri Brahmananda Sarasvati (Ramamurti S. Mishra, M.D.). *The Yoga
Sutras of Patanjali: Sanskrit Text with Translation*. Monroe, NY:
Baba Bhagavandas Publication Trust. 2010.

About the Author

Danielle Gault, with her great zest for life and learning, successfully blends her credentials in Psychology and Human Resources Management with her training in the Myers-Briggs Personality Type Indicator®, Neurolinguistic Programming, and Life Coaching along with her training in the natural healing arts such as Yoga (she was a longtime student of Yogi Shri Brahmananda Sarasvati) and Reflexology, in which she is recognized as one of Canada's leading instructors.

Danielle has conducted workshops for Fortune 500 companies, small businesses, and non-profit organizations in Canada, the United States, New Zealand, Romania, and Greece.

Her first book, *Natural to My Soul*, is a practical guide of spiritual insights and tools for self-knowledge, healing, and health. Her second book, *You as an Independent Business Person in the Natural Healing Arts*, is a how-to guide for a successful healing-arts business.

Danielle is listed in Stanford *Who's Who*. She is an Expert Author with *Ezine Articles* and also publishes features with *Self-Growth* and *Canadian HR Reporter*.

For information on training programs, certification courses, workshops, seminars, and publications, please go to: www.corporate-training-services.com

Danielle is excited to share with you in this book her thirty years of discovery and application of insights and tools to maintain balance in your life. Enjoy the journey!

Scan here to follow us on Facebook

CPSIA information can be obtained
at www.ICGtesting.com
Printed in the USA
LVOW08s1300160617
538392LV00003B/187/P